Tribal Farmwomen in Livelihood Dealings

Tribal Farmwomen in Livelihood Dealings

Author
Dr. Nikulsinh Madhusinh Chauhan

2014
BIOTECH BOOKS®

ISBN 978-81-7622-317-1

Published by: **BIOTECH BOOKS®**
4762-63/23, Ansari Road, Darya Ganj,
New Delhi - 110 002
Phone: +91-011-23262132
E-mail: biotechbooks@yahoo.co.in

Printed at: **Chawla Offset Printers**
Delhi - 110 052

PRINTED IN INDIA

Preface

Farmwomen are the spinal column of Indian agriculture. Growing food has been an everlasting saga of her life. Like other rural women, tribal farmwomen also play an important role in agriculture. Farmwomen play imperative role within home as housewives in managing the domestic affairs and they work as co-partners in the farming profession. No field function is beyond the reach of women. They are at them best in sowing, transplanting, weeding, manuring, harvesting, winnowing, threshing, storing, marketing and rearing livestock etc. Besides this they are the executive to the household activities. They take important decisions in the home and outside the home. Scientific achievements and modernization are yet to make an impact on them. Keeping this fact in view the present exploration on role of tribal farmwomen in agriculture in Navsari district was undertaken with following objectives. (i) To study the socio-economic characteristics of the tribal farmwomen. (ii) To study the participation of the tribal farmwomen in agriculture, animal husbandry and household activities and the relationship between selected independent variables with crop and animal husbandry practices. (iii) To study the tribal farmwomen's involvement in decision making in farm management, animal husbandry and home management.

From this study it was experiential that majority of the tribal farmwomen were observed that they had middle age group were primary educated had household, farming and animal husbandry as occupation, possessed small to medium size of herd, had marginal and small size of land holding, had 2 to 5 number of children, had all the three size of family, *i.e.* small, medium and large, lived in nuclear type of family, married at the age of 18 years and above.

Farmwomen contribution in pre-sowing and sowing operations revealed that the highest respondents engaged with sowing followed by stubble collection, clode crushing, manuring and seedbed preparation. In case of interculturing operations the participation of the farmwomen were observed the highest in weeding followed by gap filling, application of fertilizer, bird scaring, irrigation, bunding and hoeing with hand.

In harvesting and post harvesting operations, the highest participation was obtained in nipping/picking and threshing followed by harvesting, winnowing, storage, making threshing yard, bagging, packing and marketing of agriculture products. In animal husbandry practices the frequency of participation of farmwomen was seen the highest in cutting and bringing a fodder followed by compost making, watering, feeding, milking to animals, cleaning of cattle shed and so on.

Farmwomen took a self-decision for decoration of house (79.17 per cent) and selection and preparation of food (70.83 per cent) in case of home management. Farm management was dominated by husband decision and majority of the farm management decision was taken by their husbands, animal husbandry management was completely dominated by women's self decision.

The relationship between independent variables like age, education, herd size, land holding, family size and number of children of the respondents and their participation in crop husbandry was observed positively significant. Whereas the negative relationship was observed in case of occupation, type of family and age at marriage.

The relation between independent variables of the respondents and their participation in animal husbandry was found negative for all of the independent variables except type of family only.

Navsari district had recorded 34 percentage of agricultural labour of the total workers in the district. Normally agricultural labours constitute the majority of the working population in rural areas. Therefore the findings emerged out of the study of the selected talukas might well represent the role behaviour of rural women in farm management.

Decision making is the key constituent in the development of home, crop and livestock for farming community. Thus, it can be concluded that the farmwomen had high involvement in decision-making in these segments that are important areas of dairy farming. There is a need to increase their more involvement and participation in these areas for an overall improvement in their contribution in the decision-making process. Hence, training of farmwomen regarding prompt, quick and thorough decision making is a need of the time for overall dairy development. Empowerment of the farmwomen in Decision making is a current need of the time in an agrarian country like, India.

It was observed that the overall knowledge of respondents regarding kitchen gardening was increased significantly after contact with KVK (Table 1). In case of Knowledge regarding selected scientific innovations regarding kitchen gardening high knowledge regarding selected scientific innovations were found except IPM (Table 2). The perusal of data indicated that Data presented in Table 3, indicated that majority of the tribal farmwomen had low level of knowledge (75.00 per cent) before contact with KVK. After contact with KVK, 89.00 per cent of the tribal farmwomen had high level of knowledge. At the end we can suggest this crop in the region is an important for increasing the income, improving the soil health, fertility and productivity and also to raise the standard of living of the tribes. However, some constraints were also faced by tribal farmwomen in adoption of kitchen gardening in scientific way. It was also studied and ranked based on mean score. The constraints faced by them were categorized input constraints, technical constraints, socio-cultural and post harvest constraints, respectively in rank order as per their perception. The input constraints were the most important constraints and it was ranked in first position. This was followed by technical, socio-cultural and post harvest constraints which were accorded II, III and IV the rank in rank order by respondents. Whereas, the general constraints (56.24 per cent) were perceived least important. These were the major constraints causing serious concern to the growers of kitchen garden needs to be refined.

The study has acknowledged the changing mindset of the tribal farming communities with good empathy building. This study strongly supports the title of **"Reaching the Unreached"** the study can be guideline for other extension workers to implement this way of extension technology for their clients. On this foundation the extension personnel may locate clients for training and also those who can be used as counselor to other farmers, the study also useful for fast conversion of orthodox Vanvasi farming communities towards dynamic farming personality. The study will be helpful to make KVK family Farmer's Centric, Farmer's Oriented, Farmer's Lead and Farmer's Friendly in the field of Transfer Of Technology (**TOT**) in agriculture. The whole stocks of the seed materials have been sold by high remunerative rates at farmer's field only. The consciousness of the farmers regarding quality seed materials have been increased drastically. The cheating and looting by private seed traders have been reduced remarkably and the area under recommended cultivars of paddy has been developed in clusters and it leads towards value addition through need based paddy production for industrial use as well as for food grain purpose. The seed village concept of the farmers have been cultivated in the mind of orthodox tribal farmers to shift their age old seed through recently released high yielding paddy varieties. It was really a big achievement in the field of agriculture to run on sustainability and profitability super high way. Some important implications emerging from the findings of the study are presented below.

1. It was seen that many agricultural, animal husbandry related and house hold activities were performed by the tribal women, but when questions comes to take decisions regarding all these matter, their roles were seen skimpy. As tribal farmwomen are the key units of the family of the tribal's' community and they have skill in talking good decisions regarding all economic activities of the family, their participation in decision talking process needs to be encouraged by those people who are involved in the development of tribal.
2. Special measures need to be taken to increase the enrolments of girls in schools and to impart non-formal education for the dropouts, so that they would be able to keep accounts and made wage distribution to labors.

3. There is need to strengthen informal tribal education programme as means to the develop farm and home by providing modern agricultural technologies. The tribal farmwomen should be given training for another productive work outside the home especially for marginal and small size of holding. The family planning programme should be made more popular in this area.
4. The opportunities for productive employment should be enhanced by establishing agro-based industries, which might be organized in form of co-operatives. The tribal farmwomen should be allowed to take active part in decision-making process. These decisions will be more rational and practical oriented.

This study sheltered the way for extension workers for effective and efficient TOT in the field of Agricultural Extension.The heartfelt efforts made by extension workers would always be resulted in good impact and feedback. The technology index indicates the feasibility of evolved technology at the farmer's field. Lower the value of technology index more is the feasibility of the technology demonstrated.This study suggest for conducting intensive trainings, FLDs and effective use of all means of extension education to educate the gram growers for higher production of gram and to get higher net return on sustainable basis.

This study paved the way for extension workers for effective and efficient TOT in the field of Agricultural Extension.The heartfelt efforts made by extension workers would always be resulted in good impact and feedback. The technology index indicates the feasibility of evolved technology at the farmer's field. Lower the value of technology index more is the feasibility of the technology demonstrated.This study suggest for conducting intensive trainings, FLDs and effective use of all means of extension education to educate the okra growers for production of export oriented okra and to get higher net return on sustainable basis.

The high-tech trainings on Soybean production and marketing technologies has changed the vision of the tribal farmers. New motor cycles had been purchased by tribal youths only due to higher income through Soybean. Five Tribal farmers were able to purchase four wheelers from scientific Soybean cultivation. The whole pockets became famous for profit oriented Soybean cultivation. The NRIs originated from this district can say in foreign countries that this Soybean is coming from my native. In real sense this success has changed the vision of the KVK scientists towards farming communities and vice versa. This book also contains Decision making pattern of tribal farmwomen, Impact of various aspects of trainings and FLDs, Cooperative societies- success story, training Needs of SHGs, information necessitates of rice growers and many important information regarding tribal farmwomen in tribal dominated areas. This KVK has proved the real role of Information hub in the tribal dominated areas like, Tapi district. This can be a model for other extension workers and all related with rural development.

Nikulsinh M. Chauhan

Contents

List of Figures

List of Tables

Chapter 3

Chapter 8

Chapter 9

Chapter 10

Chapter 11

Chapter 12

Chapter 13

Chapter 14

Chapter 15

Chapter 16

Chapter 17

Chapter 18

Chapter 19

Chapter 20

Chapter 1
Abstract

1.1 Abstract of Research

Farmwomen are the backbone of Indian agriculture. Growing food has been an interminable saga of her life. Like other rural women, tribal farmwomen also play an important role in agriculture. Farmwomen play vital role within home as housewives in managing the domestic affairs and they work as co-partners in the farming profession. No field operation is beyond the reach of women. They are at them best in sowing, transplanting, weeding, manuring, harvesting, winnowing, threshing, storing, marketing and rearing livestock etc. Besides this they are the manager to the household activities. They take important decisions in the home and outside the home. Scientific achievements and modernization are yet to make an impact on them. Keeping this fact in view the present investigation on role of tribal farmwomen in agriculture in Navsari district was undertaken with following objectives. (i) To study the socio-economic characteristics of the tribal farmwomen. (ii) To study the participation of the tribal farmwomen in agriculture, animal husbandry and household activities and the relationship between selected independent variables with crop and animal husbandry practices. (iii) To study the tribal farmwomen's involvement in decision making in farm management, animal husbandry and home management.

From this study it was observed that majority of the tribal farmwomen were observed that they had middle age group were primary educated had household, farming and animal husbandry as occupation, possessed small to medium size of herd, had marginal and small size of land holding, had 2 to 5 number of children, had all the three size of family, *i.e.* small, medium and large, lived in nuclear type of family, married at the age of 18 years and above.

A View of Tribal Farmwomen

Farmwomen participation in pre-sowing and sowing operations revealed that the highest respondents engaged with sowing followed by stubble collection, clode crushing, manuring and seedbed preparation. In case of interculturing operations the participation of the farmwomen were observed the highest in weeding followed by gap filling, application of fertilizer, bird scaring, irrigation, bunding and hoeing with hand.

In harvesting and post harvesting operations, the highest participation was obtained in nipping/picking and threshing followed by harvesting, winnowing, storage, making threshing yard, bagging, packing and marketing of agriculture products.

In animal husbandry practices the frequency of participation of farmwomen was seen the highest in cutting and bringing a fodder followed by compost making, watering, feeding, milking to animals, cleaning of cattle shed and so on.

Farmwomen took a self-decision for decoration of house (79.17 per cent) and selection and preparation of food (70.83 per cent) in case of home management. Farm management was dominated by husband decision and majority of the farm management decision was taken by their husbands, animal husbandry management was completely dominated by women's self decision.

The relationship between independent variables like age, education, herd size, land holding, family size and number of children of the respondents and their participation in crop husbandry was observed positively significant. Whereas the negative relationship was observed in case of occupation, type of family and age at marriage.

The relation between independent variables of the respondents and their participation in animal husbandry was found negative for all of the independent variables except type of family only.

Navsari district had recorded 34 percentage of agricultural labour of the total workers in the district. Normally agricultural labours constitute the majority of the working population in rural areas. Therefore the findings emerged out of the study of the selected talukas might well represent the role behaviour of rural women in farm management.

1.2 Objective of the Study

The research study is designed with an objective to explore the multidimensional roles and participation of tribal farmwomen of the Navsari district of Gujarat state in general and with following objectives in particular.

(i) To study the Socio-economic characteristics of the tribal farmwomen.

(ii) To study the participation of the tribal farmwomen in agriculture, animal husbandry and household activities and the relationship between selected independent variables with crop and animal husbandry practices.

(iii) To study the tribal farmwomen's involvement in decision making for home management, farm management and animal husbandry practices.

1.3 Introduction

Farmwomen are the backbone of Indian agriculture. Growing food has been an interminable saga of her life. Like other rural women tribal women also play an important role in agriculture. Even cultural anthropological literature suggests that agriculture is invention of women. Farming in India is mainly a family occupation. Most of the family members are acutely engaged in farming. At present when the farm technology is changing at faster speed a farmer has to adopt this in order to become a competitive and efficient farmer. The change in farming has increased manifold. The farming capabilities for taking timely and judicious decisions by the farm families have a direct bearing on the agricultural development in country. It is well known fact that decision is the heart of management. Much of success of farm families depends upon how well the family members develop skills in decision making.

In India as per 2001 census out of the total 496 million of rural female population 23.9 per cent are workers and about 87 per cent female workers are found in agriculture. There has been little realization about the contribution of women in the economic activities of a country. This was a position in most of counties till recently and India is no exception.

Farmwomen play vital role within home as housewives in managing the domestic affairs and they work as co-partners in the farming profession. No operation in field is beyond them. They are best in sowing, transplanting, weeding, manuring, harvesting, winnowing, threshing, storing, marketing and rearing livestock etc. Besides they are the manager to the household activities. They take important decision in home and outside the home. Scientific achievements and modernization are yet to make an impact on them.

It is to be noted that the perception of the place of women in rural economy of a country is largely conditioned by overall socio-economic and cultural situation prevailing there. It holds all the more true for a developing country like India.

From ancient times women have played a pivoted role in agriculture. In family the closest associate of a farmer is his wife. It is natural that farmers' wives can play a very effective role in improving the farming; they contribute one third labour force required for farming operations and allied enterprises. Women in villages spend for every minute of their working hours. Their hard lives start early in morning. They work in the house and then rushing off the work for 6-8 hours on the farm. In addition to participation in farm activities and the physical work, in joint families not only wives but also the mothers have a large part in decision-making. Women's contribution

1 Tribal Farmwomen in Paddy Cultivation

Tribal Farmwomen Nourish the Society

to the farm sector has largely been ignored and inadequately understood in our country.

It is said that if you educate a man, you educate an individual and if you educate a women, you educate a family. This old proverbs holds true today with their contribution and influence remaining unchallenged. Women in the present age are facing the most challenging situation of performing their roles in outside the home for social and economic development of the nation. Farm and home are inseparable in India.

Agriculture is a predominant sector, which provides employment in rural areas. The female population constitutes nearly half of the total population. It is a well recognized fact that more than 60 per cent of agricultural operations have been traditionally handled by women. In hilly areas where men migrate to agricultural operations including crop planning and marketing of produce. In other area men are reluctant to share control with women. The contribution of women to the farm sector has largely been ignored and inadequately understood in the Indian context.

Though women play different roles in their home activities as wives, as mothers and as homemakers, they also play a pivotal role in agriculture and livestock management. They still continued to share number of farm operations with men from early ages of invention of agriculture to the present day of modern agriculture.

Empowering the Tribal Farmwomen through "*Panchamrut*"

Woman as leaders woman have been an integral part of social structure not only because of their importance in the perpetuation of human race but also by virtue of their significant contribution to socio-economic progress. The place of rural women in India in Socio-economic and political spheres in more depressed than that of urban counter parts. Although the rural woman have been contributing significantly to the social and economic progress of the country. Their participation in development programmes is onl contributors.

Looking the significant role of tribal women in agriculture and allied activities, the study on rural woman's role in farm management was undertaken keeping in view of the increasing importance of involvement of rural women in agricultural production programmes. Studies in this field so far have exhibited a little concern on rural woman's role in Gujarat state. Hence this study was conducted with an objective of ascertaining the role expectations and role performance of rural women in farm management.

1.4 The Few Words for Woman

In ancient India, women have been as less than a divine status. Laxmi, Durga and Saraswati are the three great Goddesses of prosperity, power and wisdom, respectively. The ancient scriptures declare that god lives where women are worshipped. Surprisingly the Sanskrit word ***"ABALA "*** is routinely used with reference to woman as weaker woman. The term *"ABALA"* is made up to two parts *A* (without) and *BALA* (strength). Thus literally it means without strength. However, the term can notes weakness rather than absence of strength.

The terminology is close that Manu, who saw women as dependents whom, he advised to function under the guardianship of father before marriage of the husband after marriage and the sons in widowhood.

Gandhiji explained women as pillars of strength, pride and faith. Gandhiji had deep faith on the strength of women in national struggle for freedom as a powerful moral force in society and less concerned with improving their status. It should have formed the base of post independences planning for women, as partners got lost in constitutional designation of woman a weaker section. He once said "Women are the companion of man, gifted with equal mental capabilities. She has the right to participate in the minute details of the activities of man. She has the same right of freedom and liberty as man has. The woman is key co-partner in her husband's method of agriculture and animal husbandry for solving the economic and nutritional problems of India" (Devdas *et al.*, 1972).

Painstaking of Farmwomen

1.5 Review of Literature

Gasson (1980) reported that women have significant role in British agriculture by maintaining and reproducing the labour force, assisting in farm production, decision-making and business administration and helping to improve the quality of life in rural areas. Women have three ideal role types, distinguished by frequency of manual work, responsibility for farm enterprises, division of labour between husband and wife.

Rattin (1983) reported that women represent 46 per cent of the total agricultural population in France, 6 per cent of are farmers themselves, 46 per cent are wives of farmers, 47 per cent are other family member and 1 per cent are analysed as are certain socio-demographic data the number of women running farms has gone up 1 per cent annually since 1975 and in 1981, 10 per cent of farms run by women.

Oxman (1983) aims to describe the characteristics of peasant women's organizations and degree of women's participation in them. He described the role of women in the field of traditional agriculture, the emergence of agrarian organizations and intermittent participation of the peasant woman and her restricted political participation.

Saxena and Bhatnagar (1985) reported that in Rajasthan during peak season tribal women spent 14.66 hours on daily activities, out of which 8.24 hours were spent on agricultural work and 6.42 hours on home activities whereas, non-tribal women spent 8.14 hours on farm activities and 7.61 hours on home activities totaling 15.75 hours per day.

Sisodiya (1985) indicated that job traditionally done by the farmwomen in the Chmbal region in order of importance were mainly the harvesting, threshing, hoeing, weeding, winnowing and miscellaneous work which together accounted in 86.85 per cent and 79.08 percent in 1982-83 and 1977-78, respectively.

Malkit and Sharma (1985) reported that dominance of female as the main caretaker of animals was prevalent in all regions but the maximum number was observed in backward region as compared to advance region.

Badiger and Rao (1985) found that the farmwomen participated independently more in home area, while their husband's independent participation was almost the same in both farm and home areas. Joint decisions were high in both areas, being somewhat greater in farm than in home areas.

Vagani (1987) revealed that during ordinary days, the farmwomen belonging to small, medium and big size land holding spent 2.00 hours, 3.00 hours and more than 3.00 hours respectively on their own farm.

Patel *et al.* (1987) reported that farmwomen participated in gap filling, harvesting, threshing, thinning and grain storage etc. They also reported that major activities performed by farmwomen in dairying were cutting and bringing green fodder, shed cleaning, bath to cattle, milking, watering and feeding to animal etc.

Lepcha (1987) reported that majority of the farmwomen made their own decision on storage of food grain management of their own subsidiary enterprises and to some extent on cropping pattern and marketing of farm produce, whereas the decision on social participation and expenditure pattern were taken up jointly with their counter parts.

Singh (1989) studied the need to fully realize the enormous potentials of the tribal women by engaging her more actively in all spheres of agriculture. He stated that the role of tribal women in agricultural production and others in stressed. Benefits of developmental initiatives have always escaped women due to a variety of important sociological factors.

Vicente (1989) stated the role of women in agriculture is usually relegated to the status of farmer's wife or unskilled manual worker. Recent changes in agricultural sector leads to decrease the female population and increased interest in the role of women in agriculture. Women in most European countries plays equal role in agriculture and seen as her husband's helper.

· Parekh (1990) reported that social participation had no relationship with the role performance of rural women in farm management. He also stated that family income had no relationship with role performance of rural women in farm management.

Kulkarni *et al.* (1990) stated that nearly 50.00 per cent of farmwomen had high knowledge regarding improved agricultural practices, whereas 42.00 and 8.00 per cent of the respondents had medium and low knowledge, respectively.

Kulkarni and Nandapurkar (1991) stated that very few rural women (15.00 per cent) were taking their own decision in respect of purchase of seeds, fertilizers, animal produce and selection of cropping pattern.

Uwakah *et al.* (1991) studied the role of women as farmers in Nigeria. The rural women were the more likely to be known as a full-time farmer. They reported that women have become increasingly involved in producing tree crops, food crops and livestock since the end of the Nigeria civil war in 1970.

Mistra (1991) studied the women of the nishing tribe of Arunachal Pradesh. The role of women in the nishing society and economy is interesting, both in its traditional aspect and in the changes that are taking place. Hunting and keeping watch over the semi-domesticated stock of mithusns were the main preoccupations of men, leaving almost the axis around which the nishing economic life revolved. The role of women was dominant in almost all the social, political, ritual and agriculture.

Bagwe (1991) reported that grassroots reality of village women's' lives and seriously hamper efforts to develop supportive programmers and policy initiatives so as to effectively address critical issues related to women and poverty in Kokan, Bombay. Women try to support themselves and their households without much help from their men are also mentioned.

Nostrakis (1992) revealed that Sahelian women have remained largely ignored in development policy and project implementation. Research from the field of women in development is synthesised to detail the Socio-economic and context of the Sahelian women and to draw the strong link between her agricultural role and food product. Her conviction is subsequently used as a benchmark to measure the ways in which agricultural undermining her economic and perpetuating her subordinate decreased food production and increased dependency and environmental deterioration.

Salick (1992) reported the single women practice agriculture and opportunistically construct subsistence strategies differently than most tribal members. Crop density is high while diversity is lower because crops needing heavy labour are avoided.

Nostrakis (1992) reported the enormous roles of women to subsistence agricultural production in West Africa. The women were remained largely ignored in development policy and project implementation. The theoretical framework of dominant western models of agricultural development overlooks women and their well-being. He concluded that agricultural self-reliance should be prioritized in order to overcome the current food crisis with active involvement of women.

Garcia (1992) studied the quantitative and qualitative contribution of women to family farms in Spain. A large scale survey carried out by the ministry of agriculture which involved 6203 women across 16 farming landscapes, it revealed information on activities which span the farming and domestic spheres and which tend to be left out of official statistics. Women's contribution is most acknowledged, women were working over 6 hours per day in farming, well above the national average. He noticed that the women's contribution is important in rural development.

Rossier (1992) reported that the average women spent 20 hours in a week on farm work, with the emphasis shifting from stable and field work towards bookkeeping and direct marketing of agricultural produce. The women on dairy farms and with fruit and vegetable crops spend more time on farm work, as old women on mountain farms. He also noticed that women were also involved so called male dominated tasks such as milking and tractor driving.

Chaudhary and Ganorkar (1993) indicated that majority of the farmwomen participated in stubble collection, cleaning of seeds, selection and treatment of seeds, sowing, weeding, drying, cleaning grains and storage of seeds. They further added that allied farm activities like feeding animals, collecting fodder for animals, cleaning animals and rearing calf are also carried out by the farmwomen.

Thakor and Patel (1993) observed that majority of the farmwomen needed training on methods of seed treatment, storage of farm produce, raising nursery, feeding animals, milking, preparation of milk products and artificial insemination.

Everaet (1994) reported that women have always occupied a central place in agriculture but this has sometimes led to their social and professional advancement being held back. Things are changing rapidly in Belgium, the number of women living off agriculture dropped by 28 per cent between 1980 and 1991. Women spend 81.7 per cent of their active time in farms. Mainly in the larger farms, around 31.5 per cent of the women are involved full time, others are part-time or having no involvement in the running of the farm.

Habib (1996) studied the role of women in agriculture in Pakistan and stated that the use of pesticides and the harmful impact of this use.

Rathore and Gaur (1996) studied in Rajasthan, the nature and extent of contribution of farmwomen in agriculture, comparing the time utilization pattern of males and females in farm operations in tribal and non-tribal areas. Rural women work 15-18 hours a day. Farmwomen work longer than men. Most of the farmwomen's activities were related to intercultural and post harvesting activities in both tribal and non-tribal villages. There was significant difference in home and farm activities between tribal and non-tribal women.

Nasreen *et al.* (1996) studied the role of farmwomen in decision making in various family affairs. Majority of the respondents felt that the husband should have the dominant role in important decisions in family matters. A very few respondents were not satisfied with their role as housewives. Independent variables such as age, education, caste, income and family type of the respondents had no significant effect on their decision making process.

Ogier (1998) reported that potential role of women in west Sumatra in a traditionally matrilineal society, belonging to an agro-forestry zone. The home gardens are traditionally prepared by the women. He reported that development of agro-forestry activities are traditionally female dominated in the world.

Sinn *et al.* (1999) reported the role of women in agricultural sector, especially as keepers of small livestock such as sheep and goats, greatly increases worldwide food security by improving the health and livelihood of individual families. They further stated that while women are the mainstay of small scale agriculture, farm labour force and day to day family subsistence. They have more difficulties than men in giving access to resources such as land and credit and other productivity enhancing inputs and services. The percentage of women who experience poverty is greater than men.

Diwan Yogita (2000) Major roles performed by the tribal farmwomen in maize production activities were; ploughing through hoe, sowing of good quality of seeds, seed treatment thinning, carrying thinned plant at home, inter-culturing, weeding, preparation of FYM, uprooting diseased plants harvesting, binding of straw bundles, separation of grains threshing, winnowing, drying and storage of grains.

Antoniades and Papayiannis (2000) studied the role of women in the family farm of the mountain region of Cyprus and revealed that the women in the zone were aged, with 44 per cent being over 63 years old. The vast majorities (82.9 per cent) were at the same time housewives and farmers and only 13 per cent were fully or partly employed in off-farm jobs. Younger women had a higher incidence of off-farm jobs mainly due to higher level of education and improved opportunities to choose their own employment status.

Bisht *et al.* (2000) studied the pivotal role of women in the hills of Arah village in Uttar Pradesh, central Himalayas, India and revealed that the maximum energy (average of the four classes for the individual category of work) was expended by women on household activities (169 Mcal per person per year), followed by agricultural operations (148 Mcal per person per year) and animal care (112 Mcal per person per year). The energy spent on different functions was also calculated for each age class. Girls in the age range 5-15 and women of 56 years and above spent their maximum energy on household activities (227 Mcal per person per year and 258 Mcal per person per year, respectively), while women in the age ranges 16-35 and 36-55 expended the maximum energy on agricultural operations (313 Mcal and 246 Mcal per person per year respectively). Overall women in the age range 16 to 35 expended the most energy on average and those of 15 and under the least.

Geeta *et al.* (2000) have studied the role performance, knowledge and opinion level of panchayat women members and extracted that the majority of GP women members had medium role performance level (37 per cent) followed by low (34 per cent) and high (29 per cent) performance levels, whereas the majority of TP women members had low (40 per cent) role performance level and an equal percentage of medium and high performance level (30 per cent). Approximately 67 per cent of ZP women members had medium role performance level and 33 per cent had high role performance level. A higher percentage of GP women members (41 per cent) had low knowledge level while the majority of TP and ZP women members had high (40 per cent) and medium (66.66 per cent) knowledge levels, respectively. More favourable opinions towards their panchayat raj system were shown by 47, 30 and 33.33 per cent of the GP, TP and ZP women members, respectively. The majority of the TP and ZP women members had the maximum role performance indices of 68.44 and 90.00 in the case of welfare programmes. GP members had maximum role performance index of 62.92 in the village improvement programmes, followed by welfare programmes (59.73), education (57.88) and agriculture and allied areas (55.58).

Fremont (2001) stated that women make up over one third of the agricultural workforce. The share of women remains stable in spite of the declining numbers in agriculture: 12 per cent of women who work do so full time 1 holding in 5 is managed by women.

Lohani and Khatrichhetri (2001) studied about the women in sustainable agriculture development and environment and revealed that the Women in the country have primary role in the farming system, providing 55-82 percent labor required for overall agricultural production. Women are also the principal users of natural resources and they can play major roles in sustainable agricultural development and environment protection.

Qamar *et al.* (2002) studied the role of skilled and unskilled factory working women in the rural economy of Punjab and revealed that 29, 22 per cent and 6 per cent of the respondents were with middle, metric and intermediate level of education respectively whereas majority (34 per cent) were educated up to primary level. Similarly more (54 per cent) respondents were living in nuclear family. A vast majority had no decision making power while 80 per cent of the respondents did not get any training before starting their job.

Firdous *et al.* (2002) studied the role and status of women in Baluch families and revealed that the majority of the respondents wanted to educate their children but were dissatisfied with family matters especially concerning marriage, education and share from their family's property. According to the majority of the respondents, women's rights in family life need protection.

Today women are approx. 50 per cent of the undergraduate population in animal science (AS) departments at the original land grant state universities, but racial minorities lag far behind, in part because the schools created under the 1890 legislation provided a diversion away from the state universities (Beck and Swanson, 2003).

It is suggested that the Samridhi Mahila processing co-operative society in Himachal Pradesh (SMCS) can empower the women and assist in economic development (Sharma *et al.*, 2003)

Mrinali *et al.* (2004) reported that among various demographic and economic factors, farm size, number of female household members, and women's wage rates were found to have played a positive role in determining the demand for total female labour. Level of education was found to have discouraged total female labour. On the other hand, level of education, farm size and family income were found to be positively related to the demand for hired female labour.

Khanduri *et al.* (2004) studied the role of females in household and recreational activities and the time they spent for these activities and reported that the women spent 16.08 hours/day for household and non-household activities, whereas men spent only 6.85 hours/day for these activities. Comparative data show that women devote 54 per cent of their time each day for productive activities whereas men devote 65 per cent of their time each day for non-productive activities.

1.6 Explanation of Problem

The present investigation had been undertaken particularly on the role of tribal farmwomen in agriculture in Navsari district, such studies have not been conducted so far in Navsari district where the present study was conducted. Therefore, it was considered worthwhile that the study of the nature would be fruitful. After the primary survey, interview schedule was prepared and farmwomen were personally interviewed by the investigator.

Secondary data and other relevant information for the study were gathered from the following sources. Reference books, reports, bulletins and periodicals on the subjects published by different authors, organizations, institutions and agencies. Published papers, census data and other report from the government and other agencies. Postgraduate thesis pertaining to similar or relevant studies conducted elsewhere.

Women as Gruh Laxmi

In Navsari district among 5 tribal talukas, two talukas were selected randomly. Three villages from each taluka were selected. Total six villages were selected; from each village 20 tribal farmwomen were selected with the help of random sampling method. Thus the sample consisted of 120 tribal farmwomen. A schedule was prepared in light of objectives of the study and respondents were individually interviewed. The data were analyzed in the light of objectives.

In this connection Jawaharlal Nehru once said: "In order to awaken the people. It is the women who have to be awakened. Once she is on move the family moves, the village moves the nation moves". (Hiranand and Kumar, 1980). Therefore, this problem is planned to understand the role of tribal farmwomen in agriculture, home and livestock management in Navsari district of Gujarat state.

1.7 Scope of the Study

The present study will generate useful information on various aspects of involvement of tribal farmwomen in different farm and off farm activities and decision-making. This investigation is of great significance in creating data base fuller understanding of the existing situation and also for the course of action to be taken in future. Providing an insight into a typical agrarian profile of tribal farmwomen, this study will suggest several implications to policy makers, planners, administrators, scientist and change agents for transforming an agricultural based rural society.

1.8 Limitation of the Study

Time, money and availability of skill are the main constraints. The present study has been restricted as under.

(i) The area of the study was limited to only two talukas of Navsari district of Gujarat state.

(ii) The study was confined only to one hundred and twenty tribal farmwomen of the selected area.

(iii) The study was based on individual's perception and expressed opinion.

However, proper care and considerate thought have been exercised in making the study as empirical and systematic as possible.

Chapter 2
Research Methodology

The purpose of this section of the assignment is to describe the procedure followed for carrying out this study.

2.1 Plan of the study
2.2 Location of the study
2.3 Selection of the villages
2.4 Selection of the respondents
2.5 Construction of the interview schedule
2.6 Pre-testing of the schedule
2.7 Collection of the data
2.8 Research design
2.9 Derivation of hypothesis
2.10 Statistical tools and techniques used in analysis of data
2.11 Selection of the variables

2.1 Plan of the Study

The study was intended to call attention to the participation, awareness, training needs and constraints of the farmwomen in different faces of agriculture and home activities. Very few research studies have conducted on the contribution of women is in paucity.

Therefore, it was planned to investigate the woman's role and participation in agricultural activities.

2.2 Location of the Study

The presented investigation was carried out in the Navsari district of the Gujarat state, which is one of the tribal districts of the state. In selecting the district the main consideration was the agriculture as the main occupation of people living in such villages. Agriculture was the most important occupation of the people of the district and paddy was the main food crop produced. The other important crops grown are sugarcane, jowar, ragi, wheat, cotton, oilseed, pulses, vegetables and fruit crops *viz.*, mango, banana and sapota.

2.3 Selection of the Villages

From the Navsari district, the six villages namely Adada, Aat, Chhapra, Hansapor, Matwad and Mogar were randomly selection for the study.

2.4 Selection of the Respondents

For the present study, from total selected 6 tribal dominated villages, 120 respondents were selected. To select respondents from the each village, help of officials and local people was taken. With the help of the list received from the officials a separate list of tribal farm families of each village was prepared. Further from the same list of tribal farm families, the tribal women who were decision makers and within the age group of 20-55 years were screened out. Finally by using random sampling technique, 20 respondents from each village were selected, thus a random sample of 120 respondents was selected for the study.

2.5 Construction of Interview Schedule

Due to high illiteracy among tribal women in the district, interview schedule was the only feasible method for gathering information from the respondents; firstly the structured interview schedule keeping in view the objectives of the study was prepared in English. The developed schedule was then translated in Gujarati for data collection from the respondents.

2.6 Pre-testing of Schedule

An interview schedule was pre-tested with ten tribal women of villages, which were not selected in the sample. Based on pre-testing, necessary modifications were made and the revised interview schedule was used for final data collection. An interview schedule was used for the final data collection. An interview schedule used for this study is appended.

2.7 Collection of the Data

Data were collected by arranging personal interview from the total selected 120 tribal farmwomen. The respondents were individually interviewed either at their homes or at their farms. At the time of interview, all possible efforts were made to develop rapport with them. The aims and objectives of the study were explained to them with a view to facilitating them in giving correct response. The questions from the schedule were asked to them one by one and their responses were recorded in the schedule. The data were collected during the month of March 2005.

Personal Interview of Tribal Farmwomen

2.8 Research Design

As the study was concerned to find out the role performance of farmwomen in agriculture, ex-post-facto research design was used for this study. This design was used because the researcher did not have any control on the independent variables of the selected farmers.

Ex-post-facto research design is systematic experimental investigation in which control on independent variable is very weak and in this study almost no control was possible. Kerlinger (1976) stated that ex-post-facto research design is worthy to apply when the independent variables have already acted up on.

2.9 Derivation of Hypothesis

On the basis of objective of the study, the following null hypothesis was formulated.

Ho – There will not be any relationship between selected characteristics of tribal farmwomen and their role in agriculture and animal husbandry.

2.10 Statistical Framework for the Analysis of Data

The following statistical tools were used for interpreting the data.

2.10.1 Number and Percentage

Simple comparisons were made on the basis of number and percentage.

2.10.2 Mean

The mean was obtained by the total number of score divided by total number of respondents.

$$\overline{X} = \frac{\Sigma xi}{n}$$

where,

$\overline{X}$: Arithmetic mean of the sample

Σxi: The sum of all observation

n: Total number of observations in respective sample

2.10.3 Coefficient of Correlation

Coefficient of correlation was computed to find out the relationship between each of the independent variable and the dependent variable by employing following formula.

$$r = \frac{N\Sigma XY - \Sigma X \Sigma Y}{\sqrt{\left[(\Sigma N \Sigma X)^2 - (\Sigma X)^2\right]\left[(\Sigma N \Sigma Y)^2 - (\Sigma Y)^2\right]}}$$

where,

r: Correlation coefficient

X: Independent variable

Y: Dependent variable

N: Total number of respondents

2.11 Selection of the Variable

The variables understudy were selected on the basis of extensive review of literature related to the subject and consultation with experts and finally the variables that are found to be most relevant to the present study are selected as under.

2.11.1 Dependent Variable

1. Role of women in agriculture, animal husbandry and home management

2.11.2 Independent Variable

Personal Variable

1. Age
2. Education

Economical Variable

3. Occupation
4. Herd size
5. Land holding

Social Variable

6. Family size
7. Family type
8. Number of children
9. Age at marriage

2.11.3 Measurement of Variables

2.11.3.1 Measurement of Dependent Variables

2.11.3.1.1 Measurement of Role of Tribal Women in different Activities

Role of tribal women in agriculture, animal husbandry and home management was measured with the help of their degree of involvement. It was measured in four point rating scale. They were asked to give their involvement in each activity in terms of "most frequent involvement", "frequently involvement", "rare involvement" and "no involvement" and scores of "4", "3", "2" and "1" were given respectively. To find out role in different activity, mean scores for each individual were worked out. To get total score of role of tribal women in agriculture and animal husbandry, scores gained by each individual for each sub items were added up.

2.11.3.1.2 Measurement of Decision Making of Tribal Women in different Activities

This was measured by collecting responses of the tribal farmwomen in four manners. They were asked to show their participation in decision making process related to various aspects of agriculture, animal husbandry and home management in terms of "Decision by herself", "Decision by her husband" "Joint decision by herself and any other member of her family including husband" "Decision not needed to take"

2.11.3.2 Measurement of Independent Variables

a. Age

Age in this study referred to the number of completed years of the respondents the respondents were grouped as under.

- ✰ Young age: below 30 years
- ✰ Middle age: between 31-50 years
- ✰ Old age: above 51 years

b. Education

This was operationalised as whether the respondents can read and write. In this schedule information was asked about number of years of formal schooling completed.

c. Occupation

It was categorized as under ....

Household + farming + agricultural labour

Household + farming + animal husbandry

d. Herd Size

This was operationally defined as number of animals possessed by the respondent.

They were grouped as......

Not owning an animal

Owing up to 2 animals

Owing up to 3-5 animals

Owing above 5 animals

e. Number of Children

The number of children of respondent were recorded and categorized as under.

No child

Up to 2 children

3 to 5 children

Above 5 children

f. Age at Marriage

Respondents were asked for their age at the marriage and data were collected. It was categorized as under.

Age at the marriage up to 18 years

Age at the marriage above 18 years

g. Decision Making

The respondents were asked about their participation in decision making related to farm management, home management and livestock management, decision making pattern were grouped into four groups.

Only self (women)

Only husband

Together with husband

Together with family members (joint decision)

h. Land Holding

This refers to the number of hectares of land owned by respondent's husbands. In reality farmwomen were not the owner of land but the land possessed by their husband was taken into consideration. Based on land holding the respondents were categorized as......

- ☆ Marginal: up to 1.0 hectare
- ☆ Small: 1.1 to 2.0 hectare
- ☆ Medium: 2.1 to 4.0 hectare
- ☆ Large: above 4.0 hectare

i. Family Size

Size of family was measured on the basis of total number of members in the family of respondents. On the basis of information collected into three groups.

- ☆ Small family (up to 5 members)
- ☆ Medium family (6 to 8 members)
- ☆ Large family (above 8 members)

j. Family Type

The family types of respondents were grouped into two categories *viz.* nuclear type and Joint type.

Chapter 3

Results and Discussion

This chapter highlights the findings of the investigation. The findings are furnished under the following sections.

3.1 Socio-economic characteristics of the tribal farmwomen

3.2 Participation of tribal farmwomen in home, crop and livestock management practices

3.3 Involvement of tribal farmwomen in decision-making process for farm management, home management and animal husbandry

3.4 The relationship between selected independent variables and crop husbandry

3.5 The relationship between selected independent variables and animal husbandry

3.1 Socio-economic Characteristics of the Tribal Farmwomen

This section deals with the distribution of the respondents according to their personal, socio-psychological and economic characteristics. The data collected, analyzed and the results are presented in the following sections.

3.1.1 Age

Age of the women is an important factor, which influences the behaviour pattern. To study this factor the farmwomen were classified into three age groups, *viz.*, young, middle and old age.

The data presented in Table 1 indicate that nearly half (48.33 per cent) of the tribal farmwomen had middle age, followed by young age (43.33 per cent) and only 8.34 per cent with old age. It can be concluded that majority of the tribal farmwomen with young and middle age were engaged more in agricultural activities. The old age groups with poor health might have reduced their participation in agriculture production.

Table 1: Distribution of Tribal Farmwomen According to their Age

n = 120

Sl.No.	*Age Group*	*Number*	*Per cent*
1	Young age: below 30 years	52	43.33
2	Middle age: 30 to 50 years	58	48.33
3	Old age: above 50 years	10	8.34
	Total	**120**	**100.00**

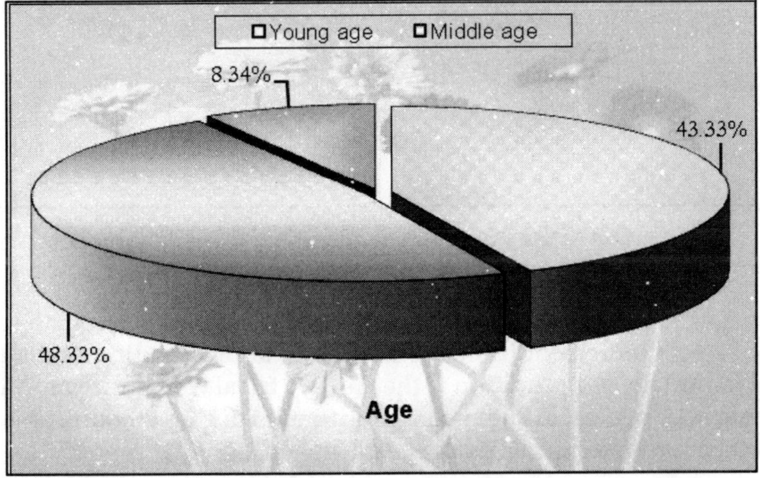

Distribution of the Respondent According to their Age.

3.1.2 Education

It is evident from the data presented in Table 2 that major segment (50 per cent) of the tribal farmwomen were educated up to primary level, followed by 39.16 per cent with no any formal education, whereas only 7.50 per cent and 3.34 per cent of the tribal farmwomen were educated up to high school and higher secondary level and above higher secondary level, respectively.

Table 2: Distribution of Tribal Farmwomen according to their Education

n = 120

Sl.No.	*Level of Education*	*Number*	*Per cent*
1.	Illiterate	47	39.16
2.	Primary level	60	50.00
3.	High school and higher secondary	09	7.50
4.	Above higher secondary	04	3.34
	Total	**120**	**100.00**

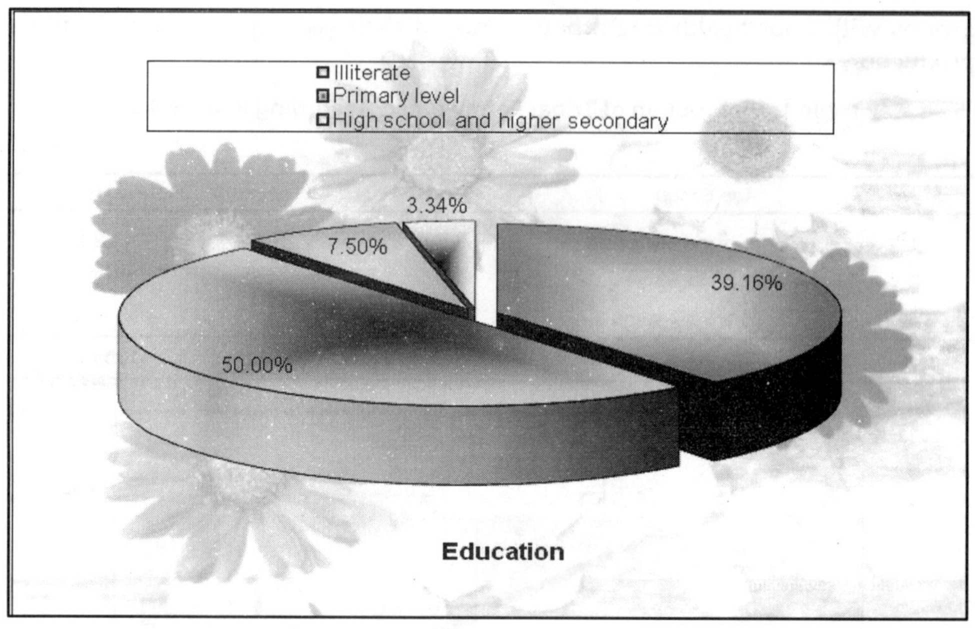

Distribution of the Respondent according to their Education.

This might be due to their need to involve in economic activity from the childhood due to poor economic condition, less interest, understanding and realization regarding importance of education in the life. The tribal women are more orthodox and showing poor interest in taking formal education due to orthodox custom might be the another reason to have law level of education among them.

3.1.3 Occupation

The respondents were asked to furnish the information regarding their occupation and the data in this regard are presented in Table 3.

Table 3: The Tribal Farmwomen according to their Occupation

n = 120

Sl.No.	*Occupation*	*Number*	*Per cent*
1.	Household + farming + agriculture labour work	13	10.83
2.	Household + farming + animal husbandry	107	89.17
	Total	**120**	**100.00**

Data presented in Table 3 revealed that majority of the tribal farmwomen (89.17 per cent) had household + farming along with animal husbandry as their main occupation, followed by only 10.83 per cent with involvement in only agriculture and agriculture labour work as their source of livelihood. The results indicate that majority of respondents were found to be dependent on farming with animal husbandry.

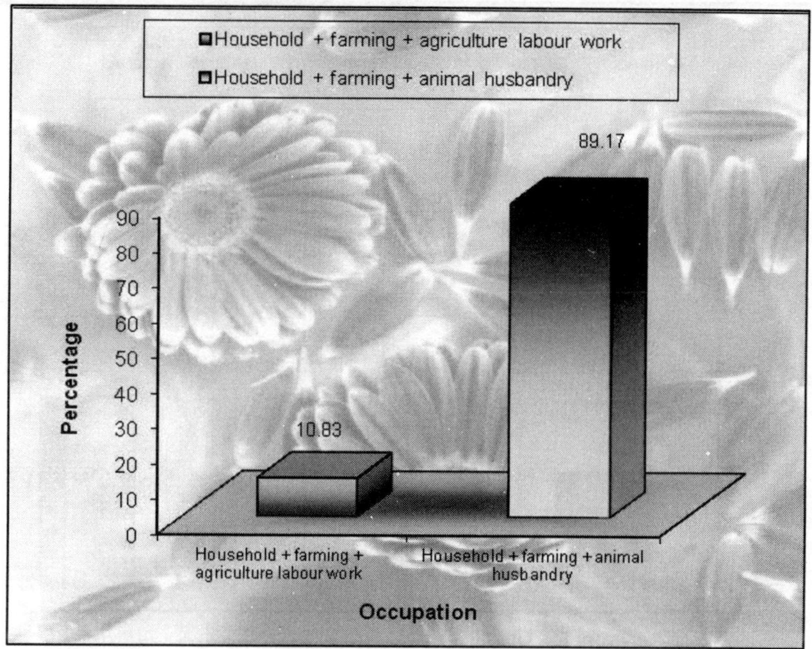

Distribution of the Respondent according to their Occupation.

3.1.4 Herd Size

The respondents were asked to mention their herd size and the data available would be classified into four groups.

Table 4: Distribution of Tribal Farmwomen according to their Herd Size

n = 120

Sl.No.	Head Size	Number	Per cent
1.	No animal	13	10.83
2.	Small: up to 2 animals	34	28.33
3.	Medium: 3 to 5 animals	51	42.50
4.	Large: above 5 animals	22	18.34
	Total	**120**	**100.00**

The data in Table 4 indicate that slightly more than two fifth of respondents (42.50 per cent) had medium herd size (3 to 5 animals) followed by 28.33 per cent with small and 18.34 per cent with large size of herd, respectively.

Thus, it can be said that majority of tribal farmwomen had 3 to 5 animals. Dairy is well developed and marketing is not a problem in this taluka. Thus, to earn additional income majority of the tribal farmwomen preferred to have animal husbandry with agriculture.

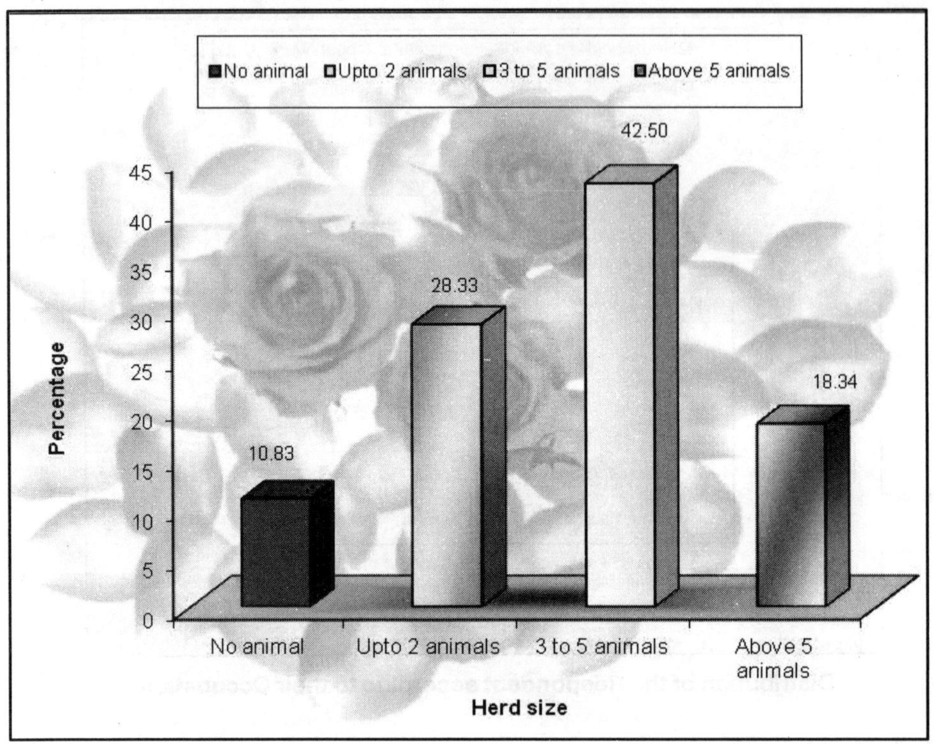

Distribution of the Respondent according to their Herd Size.

3.1.5 Land Holding

Data regarding distribution of farmwomen according to the size of land holding are presented in Table 5. Data indicate that majority (34.17 per cent) of the tribal farmwomen had marginal size of land holding, followed by 28.33 per cent per cent with small, 22.50 per cent with medium and only 15.00 per cent had large or say above 4.00 ha. of land holding.

It can be concluded from above finding that majority of the respondents had small size of land holding.

Table 5: Classification of tribal farmwomen with land holding

n = 120

Sl.No.	*Size of Land Holding*	*Number*	*Per cent*
1.	Marginal: up to 1 ha	41	34.17
2.	Small: 1.1 to 2 ha	34	28.33
3.	Medium: 2.1 to 4 ha	27	22.50
4.	Large: above 4 ha	18	15.00
	Total	**120**	**100.00**

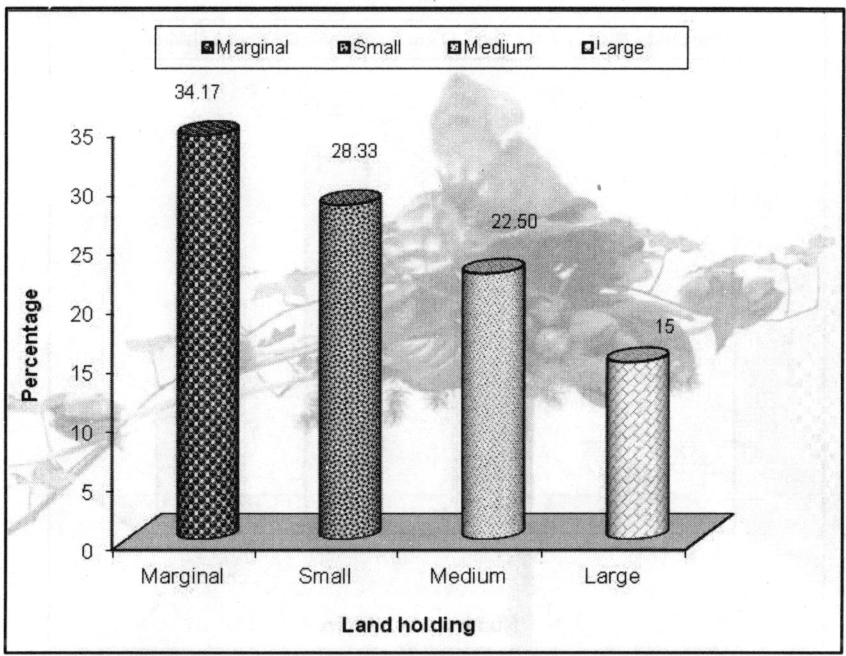

Classification of Tribal Farmwomen with Land Holding.

3.1.6 Number of Children

Data collected in respect of number of children of the tribal farmwomen was presented in Table 6.

Table 6: The Tribal Farmwomen according to Number of Children

n = 120

Sl.No.	*No. of Children*	*Number*	*Per cent*
1.	No child	07	5.83
2.	Up to 2 children	31	25.83
3.	3 to 5 children	65	54.17
4.	Above 5 children	17	14.17
	Total	**120**	**100.00**

Data presented in Table 6 indicated that majority of the tribal farmwomen (54.17 per cent) had 3 to 5 number of children, followed 25.83 per cent with up to two, 14.17 per cent with above 5 and only 5.83 per cent of tribal farmwomen has no child. It can be concluded from this finding that majority of tribal farmwomen had 3 to 5 children. This might be due to lack of awareness and law level education.

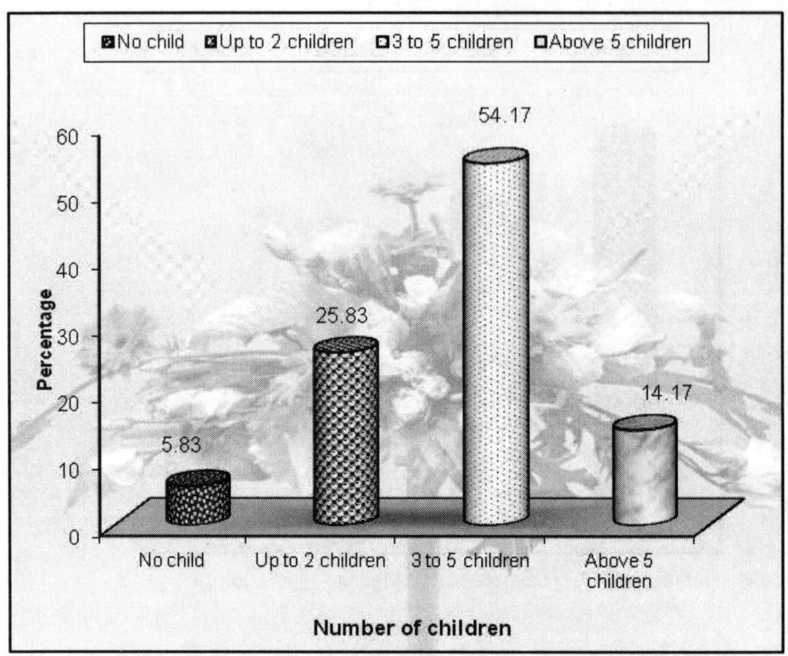

Classification of Tribal Farmwomen with Number of Children.

3.1.7 Family Size

Table 7: Distribution of Tribal Farmwomen according to Size of Family

n = 120

Sl.No.	*Size of Family*	*Number*	*Per cent*
1	Small: up to 5 members	40	33.33
2	Medium: 6 to 8 members	63	52.50
3	Large: above 8 members	17	14.17
	Total	**120**	**100.00**

A close look to the table reveals that half of the tribal farmwomen (52.50 per cent) had medium size of family followed by 33.33 per cent with small size of family and only 14.17 per cent of them had large size of family. It can be concluded that majority of the farmwomen had medium and small size of family.

3.1.8 Family Type

There are two types of the family, nuclear and joint family. The data presented in Table 8 reveal that majority of the tribal farmwomen lived in nuclear type of family (63.33 per cent) and 36.67 per cent of tribal farmwomen lived in joint type of family. From this finding it can be concluded that majority of the tribal farmwomen lived in the nuclear type of family.

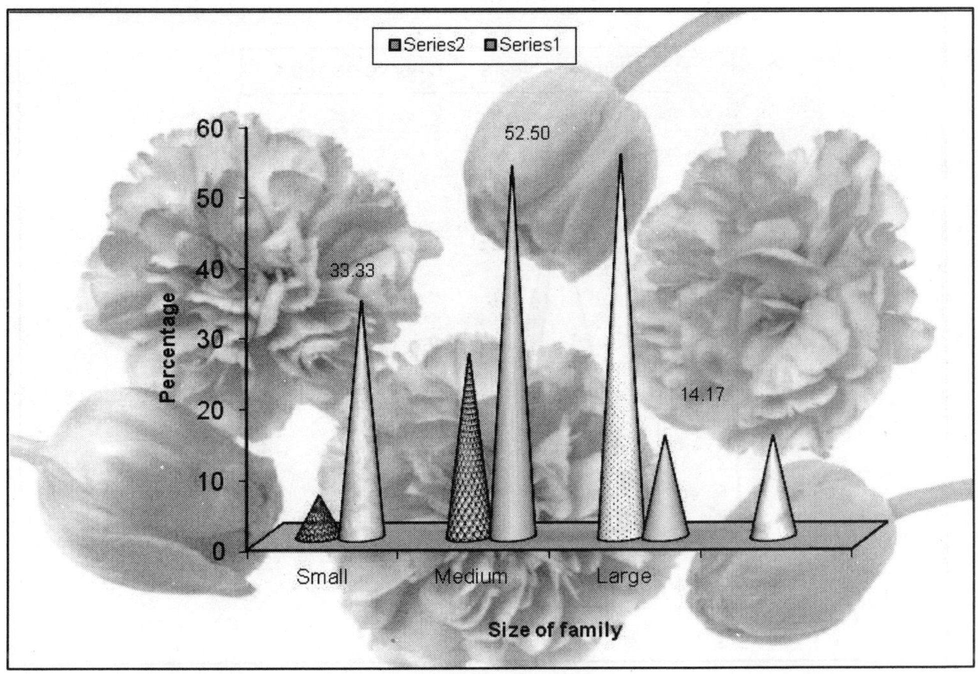

Distribution of Tribal Farmwomen according to Size of Family.

Table 8: Distribution of Tribal Farmwomen according to Type of Family

n = 120

Sl.No.	*Type of Family*	*Number*	*Per cent*
1.	Joint	44	36.67
2.	Nuclear	76	63.33
	Total	**120**	**100.00**

3.1.9 Age at Marriage

Respondents were asked about their age of the marriage. Data regarding the age at the marriage are presented in the Table 9.

Table 9: The Tribal Farmwomen according to their Age at Marriage

n = 120

Sl.No.	*Age of Marriage*	*Number*	*Per cent*
1.	Up to 18 years	68	56.67
2.	Above 18 years	52	43.33
	Total	**120**	**100.00**

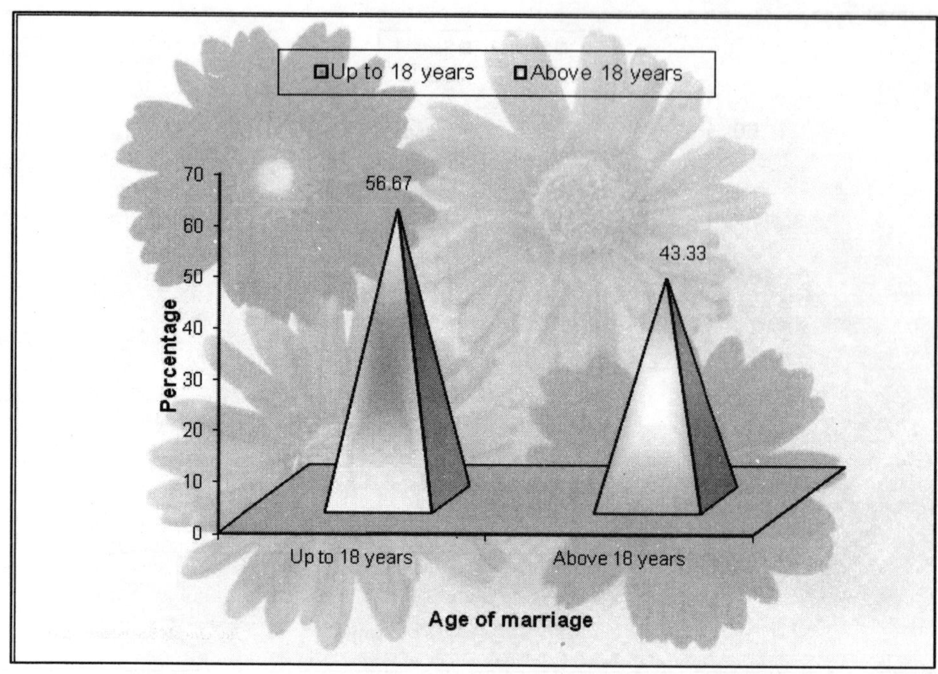

Distribution of Tribal Farmwomen according to Type of Family.

It is evident from the table that more than half (56.67 per cent) of the tribal farmwomen were married at the age of 18 years, followed by 43.33 per cent get married after the age of 18 year.

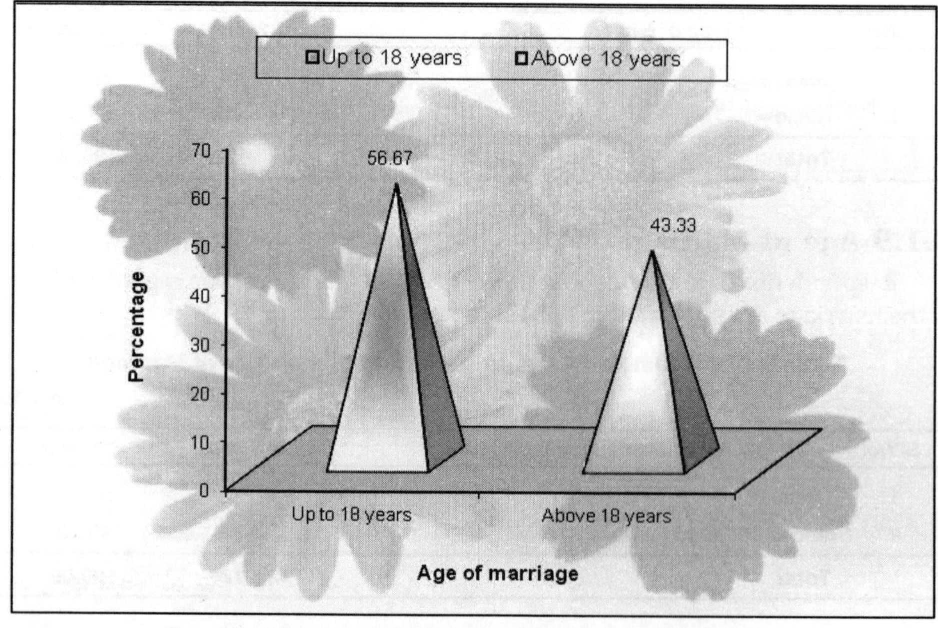

Graphical Presentation according to Age at Marriage.

3.2 Participation of Tribal Farmwomen in Home, Crop and Livestock Management Practices

3.2.1 Participation of Tribal Farmwomen in Agriculture

It is observed that when any person thinks and makes a picture of the farmers, he or she thinks always male as farmers but it is not true because many agricultural operations are performed more by the women. Keeping this in the mind, information about involvement of the tribal farmwomen in different operations was collected and results are presented in following tables.

Our Grand Heritage

3.2.1.1 Participation of Tribal Farmwomen in Pre-sowing and Sowing Operation

The perusal of the data in Table 10 revealed that the highest participation of tribal farmwomen was observed in sowing/transplanting followed by stubble collection, clode crushing, manuring and seedbed preparation/nursery.

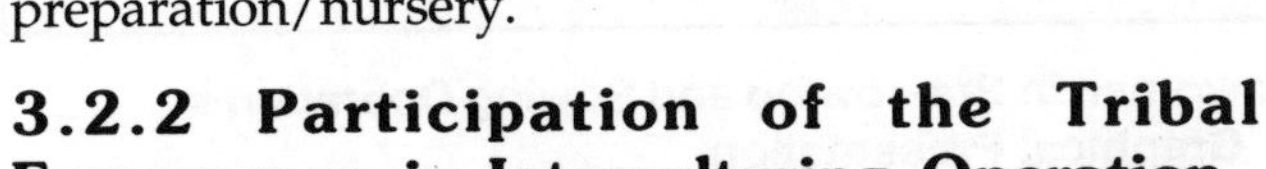

3.2.2 Participation of the Tribal Farmwomen in Interculturing Operation

Frequency of participation by farmwomen in various interculturing operations was measured with the help of 4 point rating scale. Most frequently, frequently, least frequent and no participation with scale value of 4, 3, 2 and 1, respectively.

Table 10: The Role of Tribal Farmwomen in Pre-Sowing and Sowing Operation

n = 120

Sl.No.	*Pre-Sowing and Sowing Operation*	*Mean Value*	*Rank*
1.	Sowing/transplanting	2.63	I
2.	Stubble collection	2.51	ii
3.	Clode crushing	2.40	iii
4.	Manuring	2.02	iv
5.	Seedbed preparation/nursery	1.32	V

The data presented in Table 11 revealed that the highest participation of the tribal farmwomen was observed in weeding, followed by gap filling, application of fertilizer, bird scaring, irrigation, bunding and hoeing with hand, respectively.

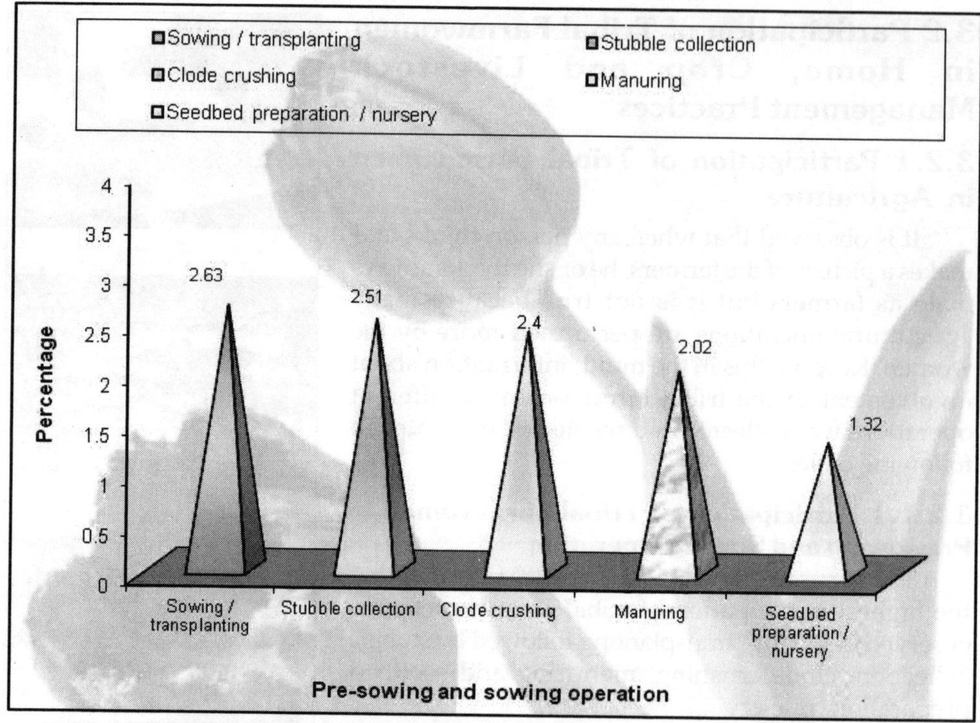

The Role of Tribal Farmwomen in Pre-sowing and Sowing Operation in Graphical Presentation.

Table 11: Distribution of Tribal Farmwomen according to their Participation in Interculturing Operation

n = 120

Sl.No.	*Interculturing Operation*	*Mean Value*	*Rank*
1.	Weeding	3.16	I
2.	Gap filling	2.22	ii
3.	Application of fertilizer	2.14	iii
4.	Bird scaring	1.69	iv
5.	Irrigation	1.24	V
6.	Bunding	1.09	VI
7.	Hoeing with hand	1.07	VII

3.2.3 Participation of Tribal Farmwomen in Harvesting and Post-harvesting Operation

Data collected from the respondents regarding frequency of participation in harvesting and post harvesting operations were given in Table 12.

Table 12: Participation of Tribal Farmwomen according to their Participation in Harvesting and Post-harvesting Operations

n = 120

Sl.No.	*Harvesting and Post-harvesting Operations*	*Mean Value*	*Rank*
1.	Nipping/picking and threshing	3.22	I
2.	Harvesting	2.93	II
3.	Winnowing	2.34	III
4.	Storage	2.12	IV
5.	Making threshing yard	1.93	V
6.	Bagging/packing	1.54	VI
7.	Marketing of agricultural produce	1.29	VII

Perusal of the data presented in Table 12 indicated that the highest participation of the tribal farmwomen was observed in nipping/picking and threshing followed by harvesting, winnowing, storage, making threshing yard, bagging/packing and marketing of agricultural produce, respectively. The roles of tribal farmwomen in all the operations were observed up to the importance level.

3.2.4 Participation of the Tribal Farmwomen in Animal Husbandry Practices

Animal husbandry is one of the important occupations preferred to have along with agriculture by majority of the rural people. It is said that as compared to male members of farmers family, women play significant role in performing most of the roles of animal keeping. To understand real picture about tribal family, data were collected and results are presented in Table 13 and they are explained in following paragraphs.

Step Forward with Time

The highest mean score of participation of tribal farmwomen was obtained in case of cutting and bringing a fodder. The next animal husbandry related operation performed by tribal farmwomen was compost making followed by watering and feeding to animals, milking, cleaning of cattle shed, selling of milk and its product, bathing of animals, preparation of milk products, grazing of animals, taking animal for bull and veterinary services. It can be concluded that the role of tribal farmwomen in most of the animal husbandry related operations were seen important. The possible reason for higher participation of women in animal husbandry would be that the most of the tribal farmwomen were possessing more than 2 animals. Agriculture and animal husbandry are the two sides of the same coin. The economy of the farming communities is basal on agriculture as well as on animal husbandry. Thus, to increase family income tribal farmwomen might have taken keen interest in most of the animal husbandry related operations. Other reason to have higher participation of tribal farmwomen in most of the animal keeping activities might be that animal husbandry related work has been giving predominantly to the female members of the family in rural areas by the male members from beginning.

Table 13: Participation of the Tribal Farmwomen according to their Participation in Animal Husbandry Practices

n = 120

Sl.No.	*Animal Husbandry Operations*	*Mean Value*	*Rank*
1.	Cutting and bringing a fodder	3.62	I
2.	Compost making	3.61	II
3.	Watering and feeding to animals	3.40	III
4.	Milking	3.22	IV
5.	Clearing cattle shed	3.01	V
6.	Selling of milk and its products	2.23	VI
7.	Bathing animals	2.04	VII
8.	Preparation of milk products	1.64	VIII
9.	Grazing	1.63	IX
10.	Taking animal for bull service	1.57	X
11.	Taking animal for veterinary service	1.48	XI

3.3 Involvement of the Tribal Farmwomen in the Process of Decision Making of Farm Management, Home Management and Animal Husbandry

In order to plan and carryout farm and home programmes successfully, there is need to know about decision-making process whether taken at individual level or jointly. Women as wives and mothers have a considerable part in taking decisions regarding farm and home. Decision-making is important because much of the success of farming depends upon how well the family makes decision. In joint families not only the wives but also the mothers have a large part in decision making. To determine the decision making pattern, the decision makers were categorized into four groups "Decision by herself", "Decision by her husband" "Joint decision by herself and any other member of her family including husband" "Decision not needed to take'.

3.3.1 Participation of Tribal Farmwomen in the Process of Decision Making about Home Management

The data collected from the tribal farmwomen regarding their involvement in the process of decision making about home management are presented in Table 14.

Data indicates that the self-decision by the tribal farmwomen was dominated in case of decoration of house (79.17 per cent) and selection and preparation of food (70.83 per cent). The husband dominated decision making was observed in case of house repair (79.17 per cent) followed by borrowing money for home management (77.50 per cent) repayment of loan (66.67 per cent) manner of sawing (62.50 per cent), Children's education (58.33 per cent), children's occupation (45.83 per cent) and construction of new house (25.00 per cent), respectively.

Joint decision was dominated in case of children's marriage (81.67 per cent) followed by selling and purchasing of ornaments (75.83 per cent), construction of new house (75.83 per cent) manner of saving (35.83 per cent), respectively.

It can be concluded that the tribal farmwomen were independently taking a decision for decoration of house and selection and preparation of food, while husband dominated decisions were matters of house repairing, borrowing money for house management, repayment of loan, manner of saving and purchase of household articles. Joint decision made by tribal farmwomen and any members of their family were children's marriage, selling and purchasing of ornaments, construction of new house and manner of saving.

A Path Towards Upliftment

3.3.2 Tribal Farmwomen's Participation in the Process of Decision Making about the Farm Management

Data collected from the respondents regarding their

Table 14: Tribal Farmwomen Involvement in the Process of Decision Making for Home Management

n = 120

Home Management	*Only Self*		*Husband*		*Along with Family (Joint Decision)*		*Not Related*	
	Number	*Per cent*	*Number*	*Per cent*	*Number*	*Per cent*	*Number*	*Per cent*
Construction new house	00	00	30	25.00	85	70.83	05	4.17
Decoration of house	95	79.17	05	4.17	20	16.67	00	—
Children's education	02	1.67	70	58.33	40	33.33	08	6.67
Children's occupation	02	1.67	55	45.83	48	40.00	15	12.50
Children's marriage	03	2.50	10	8.33	98	81.67	09	7.50
House repair	05	4.17	95	79.17	20	16.67	—	—
Purchasing of household articles	08	6.67	62	51.67	50	41.67	—	—
Selling and purchasing of ornaments	06	5.00	23	19.17	91	75.83	—	—
Selection and preparation of food	85	70.83	05	4.17	30	25.00	—	—
Borrowing money for home management	07	5.83	93	77.50	20	16.67	—	—
Repayment of loan	04	3.33	80	66.67	12	10.00	24	20.00
Manner of saving	02	1.67	75	62.50	43	35.83	—	—

involvement in the process of decision-making about farm management are given in Table 15.

It is evident from the data that in majority of the decisions regarding farm management were husband dominated such as when to irrigate the fields (87.50 per cent) Quantity and type of fertilizers to be used in the farm (85.10 per cent), introduction of new crop variety (82.50 per cent), buying farm machinery/equipment (80.00 per cent), using plant protection measures (76.67 per cent), borrowing money for farm operation (70.00 per cent), installing oil engine, electric motor and pumps (66.67 per cent), selection of seed (65.00 per cent) deciding area to be sown under each crop (62.50 per cent) and son on, respectively. The joint decision made by tribal farmwomen and other members of family were hiring farm laborers (66.67 per cent), buying and selling of land (71.67 per cent) and selling of surplus farm produce (58.33 per cent), respectively.

It can be concluded that the most of the farm decisions were made by husband of tribal farmwomen followed few decisions made jointly by the tribal farmwomen after discussion with any of their family members. It can be further concluded that tribal farmwomen had a recessive role in decision-making process regarding farm management.

3.3.3 Farmwomen's Participation in the Process of Decision Making for Animal Husbandry

Data collected from the respondents regarding their involvement in decision making for animal husbandry are presented in Table 16.

The results indicate that the selection of fodder and feed was dominantly decided by farmwomen (81.67 per cent) followed by sale of milk and its product (52.50 per cent). The decisions regarding sale and purchase of animal (65.00 per cent), selection of animal breed (60.00 per cent) and keeping size of herd (40.00 per cent) were taken jointly by family members.

Acclimatization with Technology

Table 15: Tribal Farmwomen Involvement in the Process of Decision Making for Farm Management

n = 120

Farm Management	*Only Self*		*Husband*		*Along with Family (Joint Decision)*		*Not Related*	
	Number	*Per cent*	*Number*	*Per cent*	*Number*	*Per cent*	*Number*	*Per cent*
Deciding area to be sown under different crops	05	4.17	75	62.50	40	33.33	—	
Introduction of a new crop variety	04	3.33	99	82.50	17	14.17	—	
Selection of seed	03	2.50	78	65.00	39	32.50	—	
When to irrigate fields	01	0.83	105	87.50	06	5.00	08	6.67
quantity and type of fertilizers used on the farm	—	—	102	85.00	12	10.00	06	5.00
Using plant protection measures	01	0.83	92	76.67	05	4.17	22	18.33
Hiring farm labours	—		25	20.83	80	66.67	15	12.50
Buying farm machinery/equipment	02	1.67	96	80.00	22	18.33	—	—
Installing oil engine and electric motor	—	—	80	66.67	40	33.33	—	—
Buying and selling of land	—	—	34	28.33	86	71.67	—	—
Borrowing money for farm operations	—	—	84	70.00	36	30.00	—	—
Selling of surplus farm produce	03	2.50	47	39.17	70	58.33	—	—

Table 16: Tribal Farmwomen Involvement in the Process of Decision Making for Animals Husbandry

n = 120

Animal Husbandry	*Only Self*		*Husband*		*Along with Family (Joint Decision)*		*Not Related*	
	Number	*Per cent*	*Number*	*Per cent*	*Number*	*Per cent*	*Number*	*Per cent*
Selection of animal breed	07	5.83	29	24.17	72	60.00	12	10.00
Selection of fodder and feed	98	81.67	04	3.33	06	5.00	12	10.00
Sale and purchase of animals	13	10.83	15	12.50	78	65.00	14	11.67
Sale and milk and its products	63	52.50	08	6.67	18	15.00	31	25.83
Keeping size of herd	42	35.00	15	12.50	48	40.00	15	12.50

Perusal of the data presented in table 15 concluded that the decision regarding animal husbandry was dominated by tribal farmwomen themselves as well as by joint decision with family members. The husband remained recessive in decision making about animal husbandry. Majority of the farmwomen were taking self-decision regarding fodder and marketing of milk and milk products. The joint decisions taken were selection of animal breed, sale and purchasing of animal as well keeping size of herd, some of the decisions were not needed to take by them because some of them had no animal or some of them were not selling milk and its products.

3.4 The Relationship between Selected Independent Variables and Crop and Animal Husbandry

3.4.1 Age and Participation

Data presented in Table 17 indicated that age of the respondent was observed positively significant with their participation in crop husbandry. It means old aged tribal farmwomen were more actively participated in agricultural operations as compared to young aged farmwomen. The trend of relationship says that old aged farmwomen had higher participation in crop husbandry, means farmwomen's participation in agriculture was increasing with increasing their age. Thus the null hypothesis (Ho) in case of age was rejected.

Table 17: Relationship between Independent Variable of the Respondents and their Participation in Crop Husbandry

n = 120

Sl.No.	*Independent Variables*	*Correlation Coefficient ('r' value)*
I.	**Personal Variables**	
1.	Age	0.8430**
2.	Education	0.7409**
II.	**Economical Variables**	
3.	Occupation	– 0.5553*
4.	Herd size	0.7854**
5.	Land holding	0.7774**
III.	**Social Variables**	
6.	Family size	0.8074**
7.	Type of family	– 0.6284**
8.	Number of children	0.4918*
9.	Age of marriage	– 0.8709*

*: Significant at 5 per cent; **: Highly at significant at 1 per cent.

3.4.2 Education and Participation in Crop Husbandry

Level of education of the tribal farmwomen was positively highly significant with their participation in crop husbandry. High level of education might have given

Women in Small scale industries

opportunity to farmwomen to understand the value of agriculture in a household economy. The education makes them awarded with agro-based economy of the rural area. These might be the reason to have positive relationship between education of farmwomen and their participation in crop husbandry. Hence the null hypothesis (Ho) in relation to education was rejected and it can be said that there was significant relationship between the education of the farmwomen and their participation in crop husbandry.

3.4.3 Occupation and Participation in Crop Husbandry

The result shown in Table 17 reflects that there was negative significant relationship between occupation of tribal farmwomen and their participation in crop husbandry. It indicated that the role of tribal farmwomen in a crop husbandry was observed more among those tribal farmwomen who were involving in less number of occupations or only in agriculture. It is natural that person who is dependent only in one occupation will always try to involve more in the same occupation to get maximum advantage through it. This might be the reason to have better participation in crop husbandry among those farmwomen who were dependent only on agriculture. Thus, the null hypothesis (Ho) in case of occupation was accepted.

3.4.4 Herd Size and Participation in Crop Husbandry

The results revealed that the size of herd owned by tribal farmwomen was observed positively significant with their participation in crop husbandry. It means that the higher participation in crop husbandry was observed among those tribal farmwomen who had bigger herd size. It is likely that tribal farmwomen who possess more number of milch animals will required more fodder; they need to do more work in the field. Same situation was also observed here and it was seen that to accomplish fodder requirement, more participation in crop husbandry was observed among those tribal farmwomen who had big size of herd. Hence this relationship was observed significantly positive. Here, the null hypothesis (Ho) was rejected in this case too.

3.4.5 Land Holding and Participation in Crop Husbandry

The result shown in Table 17 reflects that there was positive significant relationship between the size of land holding of tribal farmwomen and their participation in crop husbandry. It means that more participation in crop husbandry was observed among such tribal farmwomen who had bigger size of land holding. It is natural that when tribal farmwomen possess more land holding, their participation will be more in crop husbandry to achieve better yield, higher profit and higher standard of living. Thus, tribal farmwomen with big size of land holding were more active in participating agricultural operations. It means that tribal farmwomen with small size of land holding might have preferred to have animal husbandry as additional source of income, in the situation they might preferred more in animals husbandry related activities to earn more income from the available small size of land holding. Hence, the null hypothesis (Ho) in relation to land holding was rejected.

3.4.6 Family Size and Participation in Crop Husbandry

Here, also positive significant relationship was observed between family size and the participation of tribal farmwomen in crop husbandry. It is apparent that with increase in family size, the availability of tribal farmwomen for crop husbandry was observed more. In this study it was seen that majority of the tribal farmwomen had either 3 or more than 3 children. In case of the more children, there are chances for women member to engage other girl children in household activities and can participate herself more in agriculture to get higher production to fulfill the requirement of the family by means of agriculture as a source of livelihood. Hence, the null hypothesis (Ho) in this case was rejected.

3.4.7 Type of Family and Participation in Crop Husbandry

Data presented in Table 17 show that there was negative significant relationship between type of family of the tribal farmwomen and their participation in crop husbandry activities. It means participation in crop husbandry was seen higher in case of tribal farmwomen with nuclear type of family and vice versa for joint type of family. Hence, the null hypothesis (Ho) in case of type of family was rejected and above conclusion was drawn.

3.4.8 Number of Children and their Participation in Crop Husbandry

Data presented in Table 17 revealed that number of children and their participation in crop husbandry was seen positive significant. It means the tribal farmwomen who had more number of children, had more participation in crop husbandry. The tribal farmwomen having more number of children had more time for field operations as the household responsibilities can be handed over to the children. Another probable reason might be that with increasing the number of children the responsibility of tribal farmwomen increases and they need to earn more by sound crop husbandry with higher production. Thus tribal farmwomen with more number of children had higher participation in crop husbandry as compared to tribal farmwomen with less number of children. Here, also the null hypothesis (Ho) was rejected.

3.4.9 Age at Marriage and their Participation in Crop Husbandry

The result shown in Table 17 reflects that there was negative significant relationship between age of tribal farmwomen at marriage and their participation in crop husbandry. It means tribal farmwomen married at young age had more participation in crop husbandry as compared to tribal farmwomen married at old age. Hence, the null hypothesis (Ho) in this case is rejected.

3.5 Relationship between Independent Variables of the Respondents and their Participation in Animal Husbandry

3.5.1 Age and Participation in Animal Husbandry

Data presented in Table 18 indicated that age of the respondent was observed negative significant with their participation in animal husbandry. It means that with decreasing in age of tribal farmwomen their participation in animal husbandry was increasing significantly. Here, the null hypothesis (Ho) was rejected.

Table 18: Relationship between independent variable of the respondents and their participation in animal husbandry

n = 120

Sl.No.	Independent Variables	Correlation Coefficient ('r' value)
I.	**Personal Variables**	
1.	Age	– 0.8888*
2.	Education	– 0.8411*
II.	**Economical Variables**	
3.	Occupation	– 0.3014*
4.	Herd size	– 0.9464*
5.	Land holding	– 0.8881*
III.	**Social Variables**	
6.	Family size	– 0.9322*
7.	Type of family	+ 0.8646*
8.	Number of children	– 0.8036*
9.	Age of marriage	– 0.8709*

*: Significant at 5 per cent.

3.5.2 Education and Participation in Animal Husbandry

Level of education of the farmwomen was negatively significant with their participation in animal husbandry. It shows that educated tribal farmwomen had poor interest in animal husbandry related activities such as breeding, feeding, care and management of animal are time consuming and laborious job. Hence, the null hypothesis (Ho) in case of education was rejected.

3.5.3 Occupation and Participation in Animal Husbandry

Data presented in Table 18 show that there was negative relationship between occupation of tribal farmwomen and their participation in animal husbandry. Hence the null hypothesis (Ho) in this case was rejected and it was concluded that there was significant negative relationship between occupation and their role in animal husbandry.

3.5.4 Herd Size and Participation in Animal Husbandry

The 'r' value presented in Table 18 indicates that the herd size possessed by tribal farmwomen and their participation in animal husbandry was observed negatively significant. It means with increasing the herd size the participation of tribal farmwomen was decreasing in animal husbandry. It might be due to the tribal farmwomen was engaged with multi dimensional activities like household, agriculture and animal husbandry. In other words it can be said that tribal farmwomen with small herd size had dominancy in playing role in animal husbandry. Here also the null hypothesis (Ho) was rejected in ease of herd size.

3.5.5 Land Holding and Participation in Animal Husbandry

The results presented in Table 18 show that there was negative significant relationship between land holding possessed by tribal farmwomen and participation in animal husbandry. It is obvious that the tribal farmwomen had big land holding was more engaged in various agricultural operations and less time avail for animal husbandry. It is concluded that the tribal farmwomen having big land holding was less involved in animal husbandry and hence, the null hypothesis (Ho) in case of land holding was rejected.

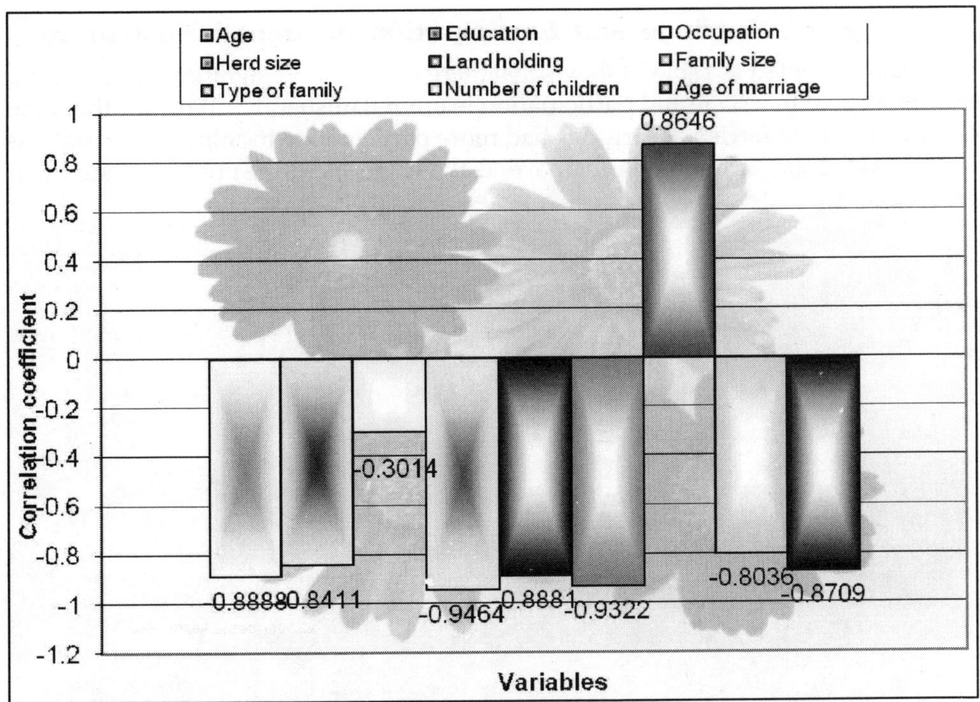

Relationship between Independent Variable of the Respondents and their Participation in Animal Husbandry.

3.5.6 Family Size and Participation in Animal Husbandry

The 'r' value presented in Table 18 shows that there was negative significant relationship of family size with the participation of tribal farmwomen in animal husbandry. It was seen that the tribal farmwomen with large family size were more engaged in household activities and they devoted less time in animal husbandry. It is therefore null hypothesis (Ho) in this case was rejected.

3.5.7 Type of Family and Participation in Animal Husbandry

Data presented in Table 18 concluded that there was positive significant relationship between type of family of tribal farmwomen and their participation in animal husbandry. It means that the less participation of tribal farmwomen in animal husbandry was seen higher in case of joint family and less in case of nuclear family. Here, the null hypothesis (Ho) is rejected in case of type of family.

3.5.8 Number of Children and Participation in Animal Husbandry

Results revealed that there was negative significant relationship between the number of children and the participation of the tribal farmwomen in animal husbandry. It means the tribal farmwomen with less numbers of children, spared more time for animal husbandry. Hence the null hypothesis (Ho) in case of number of children was also rejected.

3.5.9 Age of Marriage and Participation in Animal Husbandry

Data presented in Table 18 shows that there was negative significant relationship between age at marriage and participation in animal husbandry. It means the tribal farmwomen got married at early age had more participation in animal husbandry as compared to tribal farmwomen got married at old age. Here, the null hypothesis (Ho) was rejected.

Chapter 4
Summary and Conclusion

Major Findings

In this portion of the assignment the findings of the study have been given in a nutshell.

The major findings are summarized below.

Socio-economic Characteristics of the Tribal Farmwomen

4.1 Age

Slightly less than half the tribal farmwomen (48.33 per cent) were from middle age group.

4.2 Education

Half of the tribal farmwomen were found with primary level of education, followed by 39.16 per cent with no any formal education and only 10 per cent were educated up to high school and higher secondary level.

4.3 Occupation

A very large majority of the tribal farmwomen had (89.17 per cent) had household + farming along with animal husbandry as their main occupation.

4.4 Herd Size

Majority (70.83 per cent) of the tribal farmwomen had small to medium size of herd.

4.5 Land Holding

Major segments (34.17 per cent) of the tribal farmwomen had marginal size of land holding, followed by small (28.33 per cent) and medium (22.50 per cent) size of land holding.

4.6 Number of Children

Majority (54.17 per cent) of the tribal farmwomen had 3 to 5 number of children followed by 25.83 per cent had 2 children and only 14.17 per cent of farmwomen had more than 5 children.

4.7 Family Size

Slightly more than half (52.50 per cent)of the tribal farmwomen had medium size of family, followed by small (33.33 per cent) and only 14.17 per cent had large size of family.

4.8 Type of Family

Majority (63.33 per cent) of the tribal farmwomen had nuclear type of family.

4.9 Age of the Marriage

More than half (56.67 per cent) of the farm-women were married at the age of 18 year followed by 43.33 per cent married after the age of 18 year.

4.10 Participation of Tribal Farmwomen in Agriculture

The highest participation of tribal farmwomen was seen in sowing/transplanting followed by stubble collection, clod crushing, manuring and seedbed preparation/ nursery management.

4.11 Participation of Tribal Farmwomen in Interculturing

The highest participation of the tribal farmwomen was observed in weeding followed by gap filling, application of fertilizer, bird scaring, irrigation, banding and hoeing with hand, respectively.

4.12 Participation of Tribal Farmwomen in Harvesting and Post-harvesting

The highest participation of the respondents were in nipping/picking and threshing followed by harvesting, winnowing, storage, making threshing yard, bagging/packing and marketing of agricultural produce, respectively.

4.13 Participation of Tribal Farmwomen in Animal Husbandry

The highest mean score of participation of tribal farmwomen was obtained in case of cutting and bringing a fodder. Other participation of tribal farmwomen was seen in compost making followed by watering and feeding to animal, milking, cleaning of cattle shed, selling of milk and its products, bathing of animals, preparation of milk products, grazing of animals, taking animal for bull and veterinary services.

Involvement of the Tribal Farmwomen in Decision-Making

4.14 Decision Making about Home Management

The tribal farmwomen were taking self decision in case of decoration taking of house (79.17 per cent) and selection and preparation of food (70.83 per cent). The husband dominated decision making events were house repair (79.17 per cent) followed by borrowing money for home management, repayment of loan, manner of saving, repayment of loan, manner of saving, children's education, children's occupation and construction, children's occupation and construction of new house, respectively.

Joint decision was dominated in case of children's marriage (81.67 per cent) followed by selling and purchasing of ornaments, construction of new house and manner of saving, respectively.

4.15 Decision Making about Farm Management

The majority of the decisions regarding farm management were not performed by tribal farmwomen, thus they were husband dominated decisions such as, when to irrigate the fields (87.50 per cent), quantity and type of fertilizers to be used in the farm (85.00 per cent) introduction of new crop variety, buying farm machinery/ equipment, using plant protection measures, borrowing money for farm operation, installing oil engine, electric motor and pumps, selection of seed, deciding area to be sown under each crop etc.

The joint decision was made only in case of hiring farm laborers (66.67 per cent), buying and selling of land and selling of surplus farm produce. It can be concluded that the tribal farmwomen did not play dominant role in making important decisions of farm management.

4.16 Decision Making about Animal Husbandry

The decisions about selection of fodder and feed was dominated by tribal farmwomen (81.67 per cent) followed by sale of milk and its products. The jointly taken decisions were sale and purchase of animals (65.00 per cent) followed by selection of animal breed and keeping size of herd.

It can be concluded that the important decisions regarding animal husbandry were dominated by tribal farmwomen themselves. The husbands remain recessive in decision-making regarding animal husbandry.

4.17 Correlation Study of Crop Husbandry

The positive significant relationship was seen between the role of tribal farmwomen in crop husbandry and their age, education, herd size, land holding, family size and number of children. Whereas, the negative relationship was observed among occupation, type of family, age at marriage and their role in crop husbandry.

4.18 Correlation Study of Animal Husbandry

The relationship between all independent variables and the role of tribal farmwomen was observed negative except type of family.

Chapter 5
Implication of the Study

Some important implication emerging from the findings of the study are presented below.

During the study it was seen that many agricultural, animal husbandry related and house hold activities were performed by the tribal women, but when questions comes to take decisions regarding all these matter, their roles were seen meager. As tribal farmwomen are the key units of the family of the tribes' community and they have skill in talking good decisions regarding all economic activities of the family, their participation in decision talking process needs to be encouraged by those people who are involved in the development of tribes.

Special measures need to be taken to increase the enrolments of girls in schools and to impart non-formal education for the dropouts, so that they would be able to keep accounts and made wage distribution to labours.

There is need to strengthen informal tribal education programme as means to the develop farm and home by providing modern agricultural technologies. The tribal farmwomen should be given training for another productive work outside the home especially for marginal and small size of holding. The family planning programme should be made more popular in this area.

The opportunities for productive employment should be enhanced by establishing agro-based industries, which might be organized in form of co-operatives. The tribal farmwomen should be allowed to take active part in decision-making process. These decisions will be more rational and practical oriented.

Chapter 6
Suggestions for Further Study

1. Similar investigation may be conducted in other talukas of the district, so that the results of the study can be strengthened.
2. Similar studies may be conducted periodically with large sample to determine the role of tribal farmwomen in agriculture.
3. Similar studies may be conducted on the role of trained and untrained tribal farmwomen in agriculture and animal husbandry.

Chapter 7
References

Antoniades, A. and Papayiannis, C. (2000). The role of women in the family farm of the mountain region of Cyprus. Agricultural-Economics-Report, Cyprus Agricultural Research Institute, Nicosia, 39, pp. 12.

Badiger, C. and Rao, A. K. S. (1985). "Study on the participation of rural women in decision–making on farm and home aspect in Dharwad district of Karnataka state. *J. of farming system*, (3 and 4) : 99.

Bagwe, A. N. (1991). Women caste: Case studies from Masure, India. Dissertation – Abstract International. **51** (9): 3120.

Beck, M. M. and Swanson, J. C. (2003). Value-added animal agriculture: inclusion of race and gender in the professional formula. *J. of Animal Science*, **81** (11) : 2895-2903.

Bisht, B. S.; Bhuchar, S. K.; Pushpa, Pant; Kothyari, B. P.; Palni, L.M.S.; Pant, P; Allen, R. (ed.); Schreier, H. (ed.); Brown, S. (ed.); Shah, P. B. (2000). The pivotal role of women in the hills: gender analysis in Arah village in Uttar Pradesh, central Himalayas, India. Proceedings of a workshop held in Baoshan, Yunnan Province, China, March 2-5 1999, pp. 35-46.

Chaudhary, M. D. and Ganorkar, P. L. (1993). Involving farmwomen in agricultural activities. Kurukshetra. **1**: 25.

Devdas, P. R.; Mathu, S. and Thangamant, K. (1972). Role of selected farmwomen in agricultural operation. *Ind. J. Home Sci.*, **1**: 50.

Divan, Yogita (2000). Major roles performed by the tribal farmwomen in maize production activities. Unpublished Ph. D. Thesis. A.A.U., Anand.

Everact, H. (1994). The professional life of a women farmer. Agricontact. **257**: 3-5.

Firdous, F.; Shazia, Y. and Nazia-Malik (2002). Role and status of women in Baluch families: a case study of rural community in District Faisalabad. *Pakistan J. of Applied Sci.*, **2** (5) : 593-595.

Fremont, J. M. (2001). Agriculture in Europe. The spotlight on women. Statistics-in-Focus-Agriculture and Fisheries. **7**: 7-9.

Garcia, J. M. (1992). Women's work on Spanish family farms. Revista-de-Estudios-Agri-Sociales. **161**: 71-97.

Gasson, R. (1980). Role of farmwomen in England. *Sociology Ruralis*, **20** (3) : 165-180.

Geeta, K.; Chhaya, B.; Kalakannavar, G. and Badiger, C. (2000). Role performance, knowledge and opinion level of panchayat women members. *Karnataka J. of Agril. Sci.*, **13** (1) : 130-133.

Habib, N. (1996). Invisible farmers in Pakistan : A study on the role or women in Agril. and impact of pesticides on them. pp. 129.

Hirannand and Kumar, K. (1980). Role of farmwomen of dry farming tract in decision making. *Indian Co-operative Review*, **17** (1) : 105.

Khanduri, B. K.; Rukma, R. and Rawat, R. (2004). Role of women in sustaining life in Garhwal Himalaya, Uttaranchal. Economic-Affairs-Calcutta. **48**(3): 152-161.

Kulkarni, M. V. and Nandapurkar, G. G. (1991). Participation of rural women in decision making. *Maha. J. Ext. Edu.*, **12** (2) : 307.

Kulkarni, M. V.; Nandapurkar, G. G. and Chitnis, D. H. (1990). Knowldege of Farmwomen regarding improved agricultural practices. *Maha. J. Ext. Edu.*, **9** : 143.

Lepcha, T. (1987). A study of farmwomen's contribution to agricultural production in east district of Sikkim state. Unpublished M. Sc. (Agri.) Thesis, G.A.U., Anand.

Lohani, S.N. and Khatrichhetri, K. (2001). Women in sustainable agriculture development and environment. Ministry of Agriculture and Cooperatives, Agriculture and environment: communication issue, Kathmandu (Nepal). pp. 7-14.

Malkit Kuar and Sharma, M. L. (1985). "Role of rural women in animal husbandry : A study of Haryana". *Indian Dairy Man*, **37** (4) : 20.

Mishra, K. (1991). Women in a tribal community : A study of Arunachal Pradesh. pp. 95.

Mrinali, G.; Bhowmick, B. C. and Gogoi, M. (2004). Factors determining the demand for female labour in farm activities. Economic-Affairs-Calcutta. **48** (3): 142-151.

Nasreen, R.; Qazi, A. R. and Ijaz, K. (1996). Role of women in decision making in various family affairs. *J. Rural Dev. and Adm.*, **28** (3) : 85-90.

Nostrakis, A. M. (1992). The invisible variable dissertation. Abstracts International. **52** (9) : 3453.

Ogier, M. (1998). Possible valorization of the women's role in tropical agriculture. Unversite de Montpellier – II.

Parekh, P. M. (1990). Role expectation and role performance of rural women in farm management. A study in valsad district of Gujarat state. Unpublished Ph. D. Thesis. G.A.U., Navsari.

Patel, A. J.; Patel, B. T.; Pandya, D. N. and Vihol, D. P. (1987). "Role of farmwomen in Agriculture". Unpublished paper. G.A.U., S. K. Nagar.

Qamar, Z.; Zahira, B.; Rehman, S. and Hammad, B. (2002). Role of skilled and unskilled factory working women in the rural economy of Punjab: a case study in Faisalabad. *International J. of Agriculture and Biology*, **4** (2) : 288-290.

Rathore, O. S. and Gaur, K. S. K. (1996). A comparative study on contribution and time utilization pattern of farmwomen in tribal and non-tribal areas. **80** (1) : 87-92.

Rattin, S. (1983). Choosing to be a farming women. *Cahiers-de-statisique Agricole*, **3-6** (35-37) : 11.

Rossier, R. C. (1992). Swiss women farmers. Their work on the farm. Schriflemreihe-der-Eidgenossischem. **250** (36): 7.

Salick, J. (1992). Subsistence and the single women among the Amuesha of the Upper Amazon, Peru. *Society and Natural Resources*, **5** (1) : 37-51.

Saxena, D. and Bhatnagar, S. R. (1985). "A comparative study of time utilization pattern of tribal and non-tribal women in agriculture. *Ind. J. Ext. Edu.*, **21** (1 and 2) : 83.

Sharma, K. D.; Pathania, M. S. and Vashist, G. D. (2003). Role of rural women in small scale agro-processing sector — an economic analysis of Samridhi Mahila processing co-operative society in Himachal Pradesh. *Indian J. of Argil. Econ.* **58** (3) : 577-588.

Singh, B. P. (1989). Need for effective utilization of women power resources in India. *Economic affairs Calcutta*, **34** (3) : 201-208.

Sinn, R., Ketzis, J.; Chem, T. and Haenilin, G. F. W. (1999). The role of women in the sheep and goat sector. Special issue. South Korea. **38** (8): 259-569.

Sisodia, J. S. (1985). "Role of farmwomen in agriculture". ***Ind. J. Agri**. Econ.*, **40** (3): 228.

Thakor, R. F. and Patel. K. F. (1993). Factors related with farmwomen contribution in agriculture. Paper presented in the seminar on "Role of rural women in development" held at G.A.U., Anand on 8th Feb. 1992.

Uwakah, C. T.; Uwaeqbute, A. C.; Madukwe, M. C. and Doss, C. R. (1991). The role of women as farmers in eastern Nigeria.

Vagani, K. S. (1987). Patterns of involvement and agricultural women in household works and agricultural activities in Junagadh district of Gujarat state. Unpublished M. Sc. (Agri.) Thesis. G.A.U., Junagadh, Gujarat.

Vicente, J. (1989). Women in European agriculture. *Agricultura-Y-Sociedud*, **51:** 205-228.

Chapter 8
Decision Making Prototype of Farmwomen in Dairy Farming

8.1 Abstract

In Indian context farming is a family occupation. Farmwomen is an associate to her husband in various activities has greater role in Decision making process. Thus, the timely and judicious decision making ability of the farm family have a direct bearing on the development of agriculture sector. Empowerment of the farmwomen in Decision making is a current need of the time in an agrarian country like, India. The study was conducted in purposively selected Vasudhara Dairy of Navsari District, Dhudhdhara Dairy in Bharuch District and Choryasi Dairy of Surat District of Gujarat State. There were total 1000 women dairy cooperative societies out of which thirty societies were selected for the study. From these societies a sample of 180 farmwomen was selected by the proportionate sampling technique. The participation of the farmwomen were studied in the form of Breeding, Feeding, Health care and Management Practices. The data were analyzed by using appropriate statistical technique. Regarding healthcare practices, age, herd size, income milk consumption, milk sale, dairy related magazines training attended were significantly associated with decision-making pattern of the respondents. The age, education, herd size, income, milk production, milk consumption, milk sale, television viewing, radio listening, dairy related magazines were significantly associated with decision-making pattern of the respondents in management practices. The age, education, occupation, land holding, income, milk production, milk consumption, television viewing, radio listening, newspaper reading, dairy related magazines, training attended were significantly associated with decision-making of marketing. Based on this study, it can be concluded that the farmwomen had high involvement in decision-making in these segments which are important areas of dairy farming. There is a need to increase their more involvement and participation in these areas for an overall improvement in their contribution in the decision-making process.

8.2 Introduction

Dairy farming is an integral part of rural agricultural economy. Today, the fact that dairying is a women's domain has been well accepted. Farmwomen play an important role in performing agricultural and dairy husbandry practice and share the responsibility of generating family income. The responsibilities of all sorts of activities involved in animal husbandry occupation are shouldered by the farmwomen. She performs active role in the activities such as grazing of animals, milking, managing fodder and feeds from distant places, looking after sick animals, calf feeding, preparation of various dairy products and marketing etc. Therefore, it has been considered worthwhile to get a clear picture and understanding about decision-making pattern farmwomen, with respect to dairy farming practices. The present study has been conducted to study the decision making pattern of women in dairy planning practices and to find factors associated with decision-making pattern in dairy farming. Farmwomen is an integral part of the human Society. Women contribute one third labour force required for farming operations and allied enterprises. They have been playing significant role in Home, farm and Allied activities.

8.3 Research Methodology

The study was conducted in purposively selected Vasudhara Dairy of Navsari District, Dhudhdhara Dairy in Bharuch District and Choryasi Dairy of Surat District. There were total 1000 women dairy cooperative societies out of which thirty societies were selected for the study.From these societies a sample of 180 farmwomen was selected by the proportionate sampling technique. The data were analyzed by using appropriate statistical technique. Gautam, U. S. (2000).

8.4 Results and Discussion

On the basis of findings, the results have been presented in the following sub-sections.

8.4.1 Decision-making Pattern of Dairy Farmwomen in Dairy Farming Practices

8.4.1.1 Breeding Practices

Table 1 reveals that majority of the respondents (46.67 per cent) had high level of participation in decision-making followed by 31.11 per cent respondents were in medium category of decision making. Only 22.22 per cent respondents were lessening in low category of decision-making in breeding practice.

8.4.1.2 Feeding Practices

It is observed from Table 1 that majority of the respondents (42.22 per cent) had medium level of participation in decision making followed by 38.89 per cent respondents were in high category of decision-making and only 18.88 per cent respondents were diminishing in low category of decision-making in feeding practices.

Table 1: Distribution of Respondents According to their Participation in Decision-Making Pattern in Dairy Farming Practices

n=180

Sl.No.	Dairy Farming Practices	Decision-making Pattern	No.	Percentage
1.	**Breeding Practices**	Low	40	22.22
		Medium	56	31.11
		High	84	46.67
2.	**Feeding Practices**	Low	34	18.88
		Medium	76	42.22
		High	70	38.89
3.	**Health care Practices**	Low	35	19.44
		Medium	72	40.00
		High	73	40.56
4.	**Management Practices**	Low	25	13.89
		Medium	92	51.11
		High	63	35.00
5.	**Marketing**	Low	48	26.67
		Medium	87	48.33
		High	45	25.00

8.4.1.3 Health Care Practices

It is clear from the data presented in Table 1 that majority of the respondents (40.56 per cent) had high level of participation in decision-making, followed by 40.00 per cent respondents were in medium category of decision-making and 19.44 per cent respondents were in low category of decision-making in healthcare practices.

8.4.1.4 Management Practices

Table 1 depicts that majority of the respondents (51.11 per cent) had medium level of participation in decision-making, 35.00 per cent had high level of decision-making and 13.89 per cent respondents had low level of participation in decision-making regarding management practices, respectively. Kaur *et al.* (1988) and (2008) reported the same trends.

8.4.1.5 Marketing

Data presented in Table 1 reveals that majority of respondents (48.33 per cent) had medium level of participation in decision-making. Whereas, 26.67 per cent were impending in low category of decision-making. Rests of 25.00 per cent respondents were declining in high category of decision-making in marketing.

8.4.2. Factors Associated with Decision-Making Pattern of Dairy Farmwomen in Dairy Farming Practices

8.4.2.1 Breeding Practices

Finding indicated that age, caste, land holding, income, milk consumption, milk sale, television viewing, radio listening, training attended were significantly associated with decision-making pattern about breeding practices while education, Occupation, herd size, milk production, newspaper reading, dairy related magazines were not associated with the decision-making pattern of the respondents (Table 2). Kaur and Singh (2008) also reported the same.

8.4.2.2 Feeding Practices

Table 2 shows that age, education herd size, occupation, milk production, milk consumption, milk sale, television viewing radio listening, dairy related magazines, training attended were significantly associated with decision-making pattern of the respondents. Caste, land holding, income, newspaper reading were having no association with decision-making in feeding practices. Chauhan, N.M. (2007) reported the same results.

Table 2: Factors Associated with Decision Making Pattern of Dairy Farmwomen in Dairy Farming Practices

Sl.No.	*Factors*	*Chi-square*				
		Dairy Farming Practices				
		Breeding	*Feeding*	*Health-care*	*Management Practices*	*Market-ing*
1.	Age	13.68**	17.38 **	11.42*	13.12*	12.80 **
2.	Caste	28.32**	7.52 NS	8.98 NS	4.92 NS	7.00 NS
3.	Education	4.98 NS	25.13 **	15.45 NS	15.82**	24.18 **
4.	Occupation	3.25 NS	27.08 **	6.90 NS	5.63 NS	15.69 *
5.	Land holding	18.12*	5.47 NS	8.05 NS	7.90 NS	44.86**
6.	Herd size	0.35 NS	23.52**	13.76*	21.42**	5.05 NS
7.	Income	16.52**	5.12 NS	37.72**	38.04**	20.32**
8.	Milk production	2.09 NS	34.12**	4.12 NS	34.45**	38.12**
9.	Milk consumption	17.43**	28.03**	44.10**	20.12**	34.93**
10.	Milk sale	26.48**	13.52**	40.44**	10.18*	4.10 NS
11.	Mass Media Exposure					
	(a) Television	14.68**	15.58**	4.50 NS	13.12*	44.21**
	(b) Radio	23.52**	20.42**	4.25 NS	21.52**	23.47**
	(c) Newspaper	3.15 NS	5.55 NS	3.98 NS	7.57 NS	45.76**
	(d) Dairy related magazines	4.16 NS	8.76**	14.90**	11.68*	41.36**
12.	Training attended	4.68*	4.05**	18.52**	4.23 NS	9.06**

NS: Non significant; *: Significant at 0.05 level of significant; **: Significant at 0.01 level of significance.

8.4.2.3 Health Care Practices

Data presented in Table 2 shows that in healthcare practices, age, herd size, income milk consumption, milk sale, dairy related magazines training attended were significantly associated with decision-making pattern of the respondents. Caste, education, occupation, land holding, milk production, television viewing, radio listening, newspaper reading were not associated with decision-making pattern of the respondents. Munjal, (1989) also reported the same.

8.4.2.4 Management Practices

Table 2 reveals that age, education, herd size, income, milk production, milk consumption, milk sale, television viewing, radio listening, dairy related magazines were significantly associated with decision-making pattern of the respondents. While caste, occupation, land holding, newspaper reading, training attended were having no association with decision-making pattern in management practices. Chauhan and Chauhan, (2007) and (2009) also reported the same.

8.4.2.5 Marketing

It is clear from the data presented in Table 2 that age, education, occupation, land holding, income, milk production, milk consumption, television viewing, radio listening, newspaper reading, dairy related magazines, training attended were significantly associated with decision-making. Caste, herd size, milk sale were having no association with decision-making pattern of respondents in marketing. Chauhan and Chauhan, (2007) and (2009) also reported the same.

8.5 Conclusion

Thus, it can be concluded that the farmwomen had high involvement in decision-making in these segments that are important areas of dairy farming. There is a need to increase their more involvement and participation in these areas for an overall improvement in their contribution in the decision-making process. Hence, training of farmwomen regarding prompt, quick and thorough decision making is a need of the time for overall dairy development. Empowerment of the farmwomen in Decision making is a current need of the time in an agrarian country like, India.

References

Chauhan, N.M. (2007).Decision making pattern of Tribal Farmwomen in changing Agri-rural Environment, Paper presented in 5th National Extension Education congress-2009 at Agra, UP, during 9-11 March-2009.organized by SEE, Agra.

Chauhan, N.M.and Chauhan, N.B. (2007).Involvement of farmwomen in Agriculture and Animal Husbandry Activities.*Guj. J. Extn. Edu.* XVIII-XIX, 2007-2008, PP: 94-98.

Chauhan, N.M.and Chauhan, N.B. (2009). " Decision making in tribal farmwomen with Participatory approach.", presented in Seminar on Participatory Extension Management, Held at JAU, Junagadh, Gujarat during 31st August-2009, Organized by Gujarat Society of Extension Education.

Gautam, U. S. (2000). Construction and Standardization of decision-making scale for dairy farming *Indian Journal of Extension Education, 36(1 and 2), 77.*

Kaur Paramieet and A. R. Singh (2008), Decision making pattern of farmwomen in dairy farming *Raj J. Ext. Edu.*16: 53.56.

Kaur, S., Oberoi, K., Aujla, P., Dayal, A. and Rani, U. (1988).Role of rural women and childen of different socio-economic status in decision-making. PAU *Journal of Research*, 25(4): 655-663

Munjal, S. (1989). An exploratory study of rural women decision and activity pattern in Karnal District, M. Sc. Thesis submitted to HAU, Hisar.

Patel, M. R., Trivedi, J. C., Desai, C. P. and Patel, A.A. (1995). Participation of rural women in decision-making. *Gujarat Agricultural University Research Journal 20*(2):124-127.

Chapter 9

Impact and Constraints Faced by Tribal Farmwomen in Kitchen Gardening

9.1 Abstract

Kitchen gardening plays an imperative role for rural families to recover diversified vegetables in their daily diet. Demonstrations on Kitchen Gardening have distorted the eye site of the tribal farmwomen among health and hygienic safety measures. The KVK Tapi had demonstrated the kitchen gardening in tribal area. Since last three years about 150 FLDs on kitchen gardening was undertaken. To know the impact of the alleged technology along with constraints faced by tribal farmwomen the attempt were made. FLDs on kitchen gardening have paved the way of healthier, long, prosperous and biodegradable life of the tribal farmwomen. The results seen the overall knowledge of kitchen gardening indicated that the low, medium and high level of knowledge before contact with KVK was 85.00 per cent, 11.00 per cent and 04.00 per cent, respectively. It was altered up to 07.00 per cent, 13.00 per cent and 80.00 per cent after contact with KVK (Table 1).In case of Knowledge regarding selected scientific innovations regarding kitchen gardening high knowledge regarding selected scientific innovations were found except IPM (Table 2). The perusal of data indicated that Data presented in table -3 indicated that majority of the tribal farmwomen had low level of knowledge (75.00 per cent) before contact with KVK. After contact with KVK, 89.00 per cent of the tribal farmwomen had high level of knowledge. At the end we can suggest these FLDs in the region found an important for increasing the income, improving the soil health, fertility and productivity and also to raise the standard of living of the tribes. Anita Singh *et al.* (2010) also reported the same. However, some constraints were also faced by tribal farmwomen in adoption of kitchen gardening in scientific way. It was also studied and ranked based on mean score. The constraints faced by them were categorized input constraints, technical constraints, socio-cultural and post harvest constraints, respectively in rank order as per their perception. The input constraints were the most important constraints and were ranked in first position which needs to be solved for betterment of the tribes in the region.

Keywords: *KVK, FLD, Constraints, IPM, Impact, NAU and Kitchen Gardening.*

9.2 Introduction

The tribal farmwomen cannot have enough wealth to purchase costly vegetables for their family. The sickle cell anemia and other diseases are great constraints in the region. The main reason behind this is malnutrition, imbalanced ration and illiteracy. Krishi Vigyan Kendra, NAU, Vyara is an pioneering knowledge based institution which is engaged with transfer of scientific technology related to agriculture and allied fields in adopted villages of Tapi district K.D. Kokate, (2011). Tapi district is a Tribal dominated district with poor economic condition of farmers. The farmwomen of this area are mostly engaged with daily wages farm work which is available in particular crop season. Majority of tribal farmwomen have lack of knowledge about health and nutrition, dietetic blueprint of pregnant and lactating women and complementary feeding for children. Due to poor economic condition, they are unable to purchase fruits and vegetables from market for their daily dietary need. This is resulted in poor health and imbalance nutritional status of farmers, farmwomen and children. The farmwomen of this area are growing one or two vegetable crops of local variety in their backyard in traditional way. To motivate the farmwomen towards growing improved varieties of different vegetables to accomplish their nutritional requirement, it has been decided to conduct Front Line Demonstrations on Kitchen Gardening in adopted villages of Tapi district. Kitchen gardening model developed by NAU were demonstrated in satellite villages. Total 150 demonstrations have conducted on Kitchen Gardening in total 17 villages of Vyara, Songadh and Uchchhal Talukas of Tapi district. To improve the health and nutritional status of Tribal Farm families to increase the income of Tribal farmers, to demonstrate Kitchen Gardening in scientific way, to make farmwomen familiar with different vegetables and high value dietary vegetable crops. In spite of the importance of all facts still kitchen gardening is not a very successful venture in most of the families. The predominant reasons for the poor adoption may due to lack of technical guidance, lack awareness and knowledge factors such as seed, water, protection, measures, storage, processing and so on. Considering the significance of constraints and impact the study was undertaken with following objectives.

1. To know the Overall knowledge of scientific package of practices of Kitchen gardening.
2. To study the Knowledge regarding selected scientific innovations for Kitchen gardening.
3. To study the Overall adoption of scientific package of practices of Kitchen gardening.

4. To find out the Adoption of critical Kitchen gardening (per cent) and constraints faced by them in adoption of the technology.

9.3 Methodology

The present study was conducted in Tapi district of Gujarat State. Four blocks were selected. From each block five villages were selected purposively for the study. Among each village 5 tribal farmwomen were selected randomly. Hence, total sample size was 100 tribal women. The data were collected through personal interview. The interview schedule was prepared by keeping the objectives of the study in mind. The necessary care was taken to collect the un- biased and correct data. The data were collected, tabulated and analyzed to find out the findings and drawing the conclusion. The statistical tools like frequency, percentage and rank were employed to analyze the data. The constraints as perceived by respondents were scored on the basis of magnitude of the problem as per *Meena and Sisodiya (2004)*.The respondents were recorded and converted in to mean per cent score and constraints were ranked accordingly as per *Warde et al. (1991)*.

9.4 Results and Discussion

Table 1: Overall Knowledge of Package of Practices of Kitchen Gardening

n=100

Category	*Before Contact with KVK (per cent)*	*After Contact with KVK (per cent)*
Low level of knowledge	85.00	07.00
Medium level of knowledge	11.00	13.00
High level of knowledge	04.00	80.00

Results of overall knowledge of Kitchen gardening indicated that the low, medium and high level of knowledge before contact with KVK was 85.00 per cent, 11.00 per cent and 04.00 per cent, respectively and it was increased up to 07.00 per cent, 13.00 per cent and 80.00 per cent after contact with KVK (Table 1).Hansraj Javat *et al.* (2011) reported the same result.

Table 2: Knowledge Regarding Selected Scientific Innovations for Kitchen Gardening

n=100

Sl.No.	*Selected Scientific Innovation*	*Low*	*Medium*	*High*
1.	New high yielding varieties	09	6	85
2.	IPM	12	75	13
3.	Bio fertilizer	11	18	71
4.	Weeding	23	8	69
5.	Integrated Nutrient management	09	13	78

In case of Knowledge regarding selected scientific innovations for Kitchen gardening high knowledge regarding selected scientific innovations were found, except IPM.

Table 3: Overall Adoption of Scientific Cultivation of Kitchen Gardening (Percentage)

n=100

Category	Before Contact with KVK (per cent)	After Contact with KVK (per cent)
Low level of adoption	78	07
Medium level of adoption	12	05
High level of adoption	10	88

Table 4: Constraints in Adoption of Scientific Cultivation of Kitchen Gardening

Sl.No.	Particulars	MPS	Rank
A	**Input Constraints**		
1.	Unavailability of quality planting materials for fruits and vegetables	81.26	1
2.	Lack of irrigation facility due to scarcity of water in area	75.50	2
3.	Unavailability of land for kitchen gardening near residential zone	73.14	3
4.	Cow dung is utilized as fuel hence organics are less available	64.81	4
5.	Specific Ecofriendly insecticides are unavailable in market	51.55	5
	Overall	**69.25**	
B	**Technical Constraints**		
1.	Lack of knowledge regarding sowing time, improved varieties and seed rate	82.00	1
2.	Lack of knowledge regarding nutritious fruits and vegetables selection	74.45	2
3.	Lack of knowledge regarding major pests. it's identification and management	65.64	3
4.	Lack of knowledge regarding critical growth stages for irrigation	54.75	4
5.	Lack of knowledge regarding manures and fertilizers recommendation	53.76	5
6.	Lack of knowledge regarding seed multiplication	52.12	6
7.	Lack of knowledge regarding seed treatment	47.35	7
	Overall	**61.43**	
C	**Socio-cultural constraints**		
1.	Fear of farm produce robbery	72.31	1
2.	prejudices/orthodoxy	64.55	2
3.	Age old traditional practices adoption	60.76	3
4.	Migration of Rural youth towards urban area	55.26	4
5.	Low involvement of housewife in cultivation practices	51.23	5
	Overall	**60.82**	

Contd...

Table 4–*Contd...*

Sl.No.	*Particulars*	*MPS*	*Rank*
D	**Post harvest constraints**		
1.	Problem in surplus small quantity produce selling	69.78	1
2.	Lack of storage facility for surplus small quantity produce	63.45	2
3.	Unavailability of local market at village level	59.55	3
4.	Difficulty in immediate payment after selling at local level	54.10	4
5.	Lack of knowledge regarding fruit and vegetable preservation	46.25	5
	Overall	**58.62**	
E	**General constraints**		
1.	High poultry and monkey menace	71.86	1
2.	Problem of proper protection of local goat and cattle grazing	60.15	2
3.	Less priority of kitchen gardening as compared with other farm activities	52.19	3
4.	Frequent deluge of kitchen garden during rainy season	40.78	4
	Overall	**56.24**	

Data presented in Table 3 indicated that majority of the farmer had low level of knowledge (78.00 per cent) before contact with KVK. After contact with KVK, 88.00 per cent of the farmers had high level of knowledge regarding scientific cultivation of Kitchen gardening Asha Godawat. (2011) and Suman *et al.* (2011) supported the facts.

Attempts were also made to study and categories the major constraints into suitable topics *viz-* input, technical, socio-economic, post harvest and general constraints faced by tribal farmwomen in kitchen gardening (Table 4). Unavailability of quality planting materials for fruits and vegetables (81.26 per cent) was the most important problem faced by the farmers as it ranked on first position (Table 5). Similar result was reported by Kanbid and Sharma, (1994).The major constraints faced by the tribal farmwomen regarding technical was Lack of knowledge regarding sowing time, improved varieties and seed rate(82.00 per cent) and it was supported Sisodia and Rathore, (2004) and S. Shethy *et al.* (2010). In case of Socio-cultural constraints the most important was Fear of farm produce robbery (72.31 per cent).Difficulties in selling of surplus small quantity produce (69.78 per cent) was the major constraint faced under Post harvest constraints. High poultry and monkey menace (71.86 per cent) was the main general constraint faced by kitchen gardening growers.

Table 5: Major Constraints Faced by Farmwomen in Adoption of Kitchen Gardening

Sl.No.	*Particulars*	*MPS*	*Rank*
1.	Input Constraints	69.25	I
2.	Technical Constraints	61.43	II
3.	Socio-cultural constraint)s	60.82	III
4.	Post harvest constraints	58.62	IV
5.	General Constraints	56.24	V

Category-wise Constraints as Perceived

In order to find out the relationship between the ranks accorded by groups of respondents to different category of constraints, rank order correlation was calculated(Table 5).It is clear that major category of constraint *i.e.* input constraint(69.25 per cent) was the top ranked as perceived by the farmers having kitchen garden. Other major category of constraints as perceived by the respondents in kitchen gardening like technical(61.43 per cent), Socio-cultural constraints(60.82 per cent), Post harvest constraints(58.62 per cent) and general Constraints(56.24 per cent) were accorded II,III and IV ranks in rank order by respondents. Whereas, the general constraints (56.24 per cent) were perceived least important and ranked on fifth rank. S. Shethy *et al.* (2010) and P. Kumar *et al.* (2011) supported the same.

9.5 Conclusion

It was observed that the overall knowledge of respondents regarding kitchen gardening was increased significantly after contact with KVK(Table 1).In case of Knowledge regarding selected scientific innovations regarding kitchen gardening high knowledge regarding selected scientific innovations were found except IPM (Table 2). The perusal of data indicated that Data presented in table -3 indicated that majority of the tribal farmwomen had low level of knowledge (75.00 per cent) before contact with KVK. After contact with KVK, 89.00 per cent of the tribal farmwomen had high level of knowledge. At the end we can suggest this crop in the region is an important for increasing the income, improving the soil health, fertility and productivity and also to raise the standard of living of the tribes. However some constraints were also faced by tribal farmwomen in adoption of kitchen gardening in scientific way. It was also studied and ranked based on mean score. The constraints faced by them were categorized input constraints, technical constraints, socio-cultural and post harvest constraints, respectively in rank order as per their perception. The input constraints were the most important constraints and it was ranked in first position. This was followed by technical, socio-cultural and post harvest constraints which were accorded II, III and IV the rank in rank order by respondents. Whereas, the general constraints (56.24 per cent) were perceived least important. These were the major constraints causing serious concern to the growers of kitchen garden needs to be refined.

References

Anita Singh, S.K. Sharma and Chitra, Henry. (2010).Impact of Women SHGs in changing Socio-economic Status of Rural Families in Bikaner District of Rajasthan. *Rajasthan Journal of Ext. Edu*. (17-18):112-114.

Asha Godawat. (2011). Adoption of Entrepreneurial Activities Envisaged under Rajasthan Mission on Livelihood by Women. *Rajasthan Journal of Ext. Edu* (17-18):187-190.

Chauhan, N.M.(2012).Impact and constraints analysis of tribal farmwomen in adoption of kitchen gardening. *Agriculture Update*, Volume-7(Issue 3 and 4) August and November-2012.pp:218-221.

Hansraj Javat, M.M. Patel, K.S. Kumar and Arvind Saxena, (2011). *mpact of front Line Demonstrations on Scientific Temperament of Wheat Growers. Rajasthan Journal of Ext. Edu* (17-18):115-117.

K.D. Kokate, (2011). Role of KVKs in Developing Technology Application Models. Paper presented in 6th NEEC-2011 at Old Goa, during 17-19th December, 2011.

Kanbid, B.R. and Sharma, D.D. (1994). Adoption constraints of scientific horticultural technology. *Indian Journal of Ext. Edu.* XXX (1 and 2):119-122.

Meena, S.R. and Sisodiya, S.S. (2004). Constraints as perceived by the respondents in adoption of recommended guava production technology. *Rajasthan Journal of Ext. Edu* (12-13):146-153.

P. Kumar, R. Peshin, M.S. Nain and J.S. Manhas(2011). Constraints in pulses cultivation as perceived by the farmers. *Rajasthan Journal of Ext. Edu* (17-18):33-36.

P. Sharma and P.N. Kalla (2011). Constraints perceived by the Union Officials of URMUL Kikaner. *Rajasthan Journal of Ext. Edu* (17-18):44-47.

S.Sethy, S.Sarkar and M. Kumar, (2010). Constraints in adoption of Improved Techniques of Kitchen Gardenig. *Indian Res. J. Ext. Edu.* X (2):89-92.

Sisodiya, S.S. and Rathore, O.S. (2004). Constraints in adoption of improved groundnut cultivation practices faced by the farmers in Udaipur district of Rajasthan. *Rajasthan Journal of Ext. Edu* (12-13):91-94

Suman Khandelwal, Rajendra Rathore and S.K. Sharma, (2011).Adoption Behaviour of Farmwomen about Home Science.

Warde, P.N. Bhope, R.S. and Chaudhary, D.P. (1991). Adoption of dry land horticulture technology. *Maharashtra Journal of Ext. Edu.* X (2):108.

Chapter 10

Collision of Linakges with Tribal Co-operatives for Effective TOT in Tribal Belt

10.1 Abstract

Krishi Vigyan Kendra working as grass root level TOT institute in Tapi district. Krishi Vigyan Kendra's mandatory work of linkage between GO's, NGO's, Co-operatives, SHGs and all related to agriculture and rural development. Tapi district is newly borne tribal dominated district of South Gujarat. District comprises 5 blocks. In Tapi district the **Hangati Mahila Trust** has a good linkage among tribal farmwomen. The trust has more than 2500 tribal women members, 2.5 crores deposits and regular crop loan facilities of more than 2 crores to the tribal farmwomen every year. The said trust has multifarious activities of tribal development such as Kirana shop, Hospitals, Schools, Watershed development project, SHGs, Wadi Yojna, Land leveling scheme, agricultural extension and many more. In short, this is an imperative and foremost organization among eastern belt of Tapi district in South Gujarat. The **Hangati Mahila Trust** has good linkage with tribal farming community of the district. The main aim of Krishi Vigyan Kendra and the said trust is more or less on same line. To take and advantage of readymade display place of this organization KVK, Vyara of Tapi district has made MOU in the year 2008. A big Shibir was organized at KVK, Tapi and formulated a frame work for jointly working together. A three tier committee was formulated for effective implementation of the programmes monitoring and evaluation, documentation and impact analysis.

The 84 villages linked with this mission are on the path of drastic changes in their agriculture and live stock management, each and every problems related to agriculture and animal husbandry could immediately solved by KVK scientists. The all integrated approaches of crop and live stock management had been implemented easily. The recent innovation in the field of agriculture is immediately implemented by KVK scientist among these villages and farmers are very eager to adopt such technologies given by KVK scientist with full interest and confidence. The traditional methods of farming along with same prejudices and religious belief have been changed scientific technology and we could successfully change mindset of tribal farming communities. Which will be a great achievement in the field of agricultural extension management? Linkage with Hangati Mahila Trust was an ideal example of unique piece of work done by this KVK. The study has acknowledged the changing mindset of the tribal farming communities with good empathy building. This study strongly supports the title of **"Reaching the Unreached"** the study can be guideline for other extension workers to implement this way of extension technology for their clients. On this foundation the extension personnel may locate clients for training and also those who can be used as counselor to other farmers, the study also useful for fast conversion of orthodox Vanvasi farming communities towards dynamic farming personality. The study will be helpful to make KVK family Farmer's Centric, Farmer's Oriented, Farmer's Lead and Farmer's Friendly in the field of Transfer of Technology in agriculture.

10.2 Introduction

Krishi Vigyan Kendra working as grass root level TOT institute in Tapi district. Krishi Vigyan Kendra's mandatory work of linkage between GO's, NGO's, Co-operatives, SHGs and all related to agriculture and rural development. Tapi district is newly borne tribal dominated district of South Gujarat. District comprises 5 blocks. In Tapi district the **Hangati Mahila Trust** has a good linkage among tribal farmwomen. The trust has more than 2500 tribal women members, 2.5 crores deposits and regular crop loan facilities of more than 2 crores to the tribal farmwomen every year. The said trust has multifarious activities of tribal development such as Kirana shop, Hospitals, Schools, Watershed development project, SHGs, Wadi Yojna, Land leveling scheme and many more. In short, this is an imperative and foremost organization among eastern belt of Tapi district in South Gujarat. The **Hangati Mahila Trust** has good linkage with tribal farming community of the district. The main aim of Krishi Vigyan Kendra and the said trust is more or less on same line.

To take and advantage of readymade display place of this organization KVK, Vyara of Tapi district has made MOU in the year 2008. A big Shibir was organized at KVK, Tapi and formulated a frame work for jointly working together. A three tier committee was formulated for effective implementation of the programmes monitoring and evaluation, documentation and impact analysis. The **Three Tier Committees** are as under:

10.3 Intervention

I. Executive Committee

Members

1. Programme Co-ordinator, KVK, Vyara

2. Executive Secretary of Hangati Trust
3. All SMSs of KVK
4. Resource persons of related villages

II. Middle Level Committee

Members

1. All SMS of KVK
2. Presidents and Secretaries of selected clusters.
3. Selected progressive farmers and farmwomen.

III. Grassroot Level Committee

Members

1. Selected leaders of FIGs, FWIGs, Rural Youths and

Village Workers

2. Concern SMSs
3. Representatives of **Hangati Mahila Trust.**

The meeting of executive committee is mandatory at least once in a month. The meeting of middle level committee is scheduled twice in a month and grass root level committee meeting scheduled as and when require. The whole mission was started with a specific goal. The key elements in the mission are Tribal farmers, farmwomen and rural youth. The mission has been started with commitment to get result oriented, impact oriented and visible outcomes. As a result of this mission, the different extension activities were carried out.

Table 1: Training Programme Conducted by KVK

Sl.No.	*No. of Training*		*Participants*	
	On Campus	*Off Campus*	*On Campus*	*Off Campus*
1	6	12	243	486

Table 2: Extension Activities

Sl.No.	*Venue*	*Title*	*Participants*
1.	Mandal	Dangar Pak Parisamvad-v-Khedut Shibir	558
2.	Mandal	Khedut Shibir cum Paddy Crop Symposium	1372
3.	Jamkhadi	Pak Parisamvad-v-Khedut Shibir	910
4.	Mandal, Amji	Animal Camp	542 Animals
5.	Gatadi, Bedi, Mirpur, Ghodchit	Animal Camp	480 Animals
6.	Nishana, Bedi	Film shows–2	90
7.	Mandal/Amji	SHG Meeting–2	2500 women
8.	Bedi, Mandal, Amji	Field Day–3	287

Table 3: Seed Material Distribution

Sl.No.	*Crop*	*Qty*	*Beneficiaries*
1.	Paddy – Drilled (GR-5,8 and 9)	1500 Kg.	30
2.	Paddy – T.P.(GR-7)	125 Kg.	10
3.	Jowar (GJ-42,CSH-20,23)	25 Kg.	8
4.	Tur (Vaishali)	1250 Kg.	150

Table 4: FLDs Conducted

Sl.No.	*Crop*	*Area*	*No. of Participants*
1.	Castor(GCH-5)	5 ha.	10
2.	Groundnut(G.G-6)	10 ha.	20
3.	Gram(G.G-2)	5 ha.	10
4.	Paddy – Drilled (GR-5)	5 ha.	10
5.	Paddy – T.P.(GR-7)	5 ha.	10

Table 5: Kitchen Gardening

No. of Beneficiaries	50 Tribal Farmwomen
Kitchen Gardening conducted in Bedi, Mandal, Nishana, Amji of Hangati trust	

Looking to the success of the kitchen garden demonstrations the tribal farmwomen themselves motivated and standing by to adopt this technology by their cost. Next year nearly 200 kitchen garden demonstrations were prearranged in this belt. The tribal farmwomen from other regions were also demanded for kitchen garden demonstrations. This year almost certainly more than 500 demonstrations will be conducted in Vyara and Songadh block with the help of different agencies. The nutritional discrepancy and undernourishment will be diminishing. The use of back yard space and wear and tear water of domestic purpose would be utilized in a better way.Live contact was maintained among KVK scientist and Hangati Mahila Trust Family. The constant follow up and spot guidance as and when required is maintained by KVK scientists. The live contact of KVK scientists in the form of On/Off campus trainings, Shibirs, farm visit, field day, fortnightly and monthly meetings, ex-trainee visits, group field visits, kishan gosthis and different programmes are preserved throughout the year.

The tribal farming community has created a sense of belongingness with KVK and they are in such opinion that KVK and Hangati Trust is really working for their own benefits. A good channel was developed among 84 tribal dominated villages of Songadh and Vyara block. Scientist visit to these villages and farmers visit to KVK became common phenomenon. The Union Minister for Tribal Affairs; **Dr. Tushar Chaudhary** has also visited the villages to observe the activities and fully satisfied with it.

Our honourable Vice Chancellor, Director of Research, Director of Extension Education, All Deans and Directors and Research Scientist of NAU also contributed consciously to this mission.

10.4 Conclusion

The 84 villages linked with this mission are on the path of drastic changes in their agriculture and live stock management, each and every problems related to agriculture and animal husbandry could immediately solved by KVK scientists. The all integrated approaches of crop and live stock management had been implemented easily. The recent innovation in the field of agriculture is immediately implemented by KVK scientist among these villages and farmers are very eager to adopt such technologies given by KVK scientist with full interest and confidence. The traditional methods of farming along with same prejudices and religious belief have been changed scientific technology and we could successfully change mindset of tribal farming communities. This will be a great achievement in the field of agricultural extension management. Linkage with Hangati Mahila Trust was an ideal example of unique piece of work done by this KVK.

10.5 Implication

The study has acknowledged the changing mindset of the tribal farming communities with good empathy building. This study strongly supports the title of **"Reaching the Unreached"** the study can be guideline for other extension workers to implement this way of extension technology for their clients. On this foundation the extension personnel may locate clients for training and also those who can be used as counselor to other farmers, the study also useful for fast conversion of orthodox Vanvasi farming communities towards dynamic farming personality. The study will be helpful to make KVK family Farmer's Centric, Farmer's Oriented, Farmer's Lead and Farmer's Friendly in the field of Transfer Of Technology in agriculture.

References

Bhatt S.T. and Chauhan, N.M. (2012). Effect of different growth hormones on growth and flowering of Dendrobium CV, "Sonia-17".*GreenFarming (An International Journal of Applied Agricultural and Horticultural Sciences)* VOL: 3(3):375-376.

Chauhan, N.M. and Patel, A. (2012). Increasing area and productivity of paddy in tribal belt of South Gujarat through effective TOT efforts: A success story. *International Journal of Agric. Sci.Jan-2012:8(1):301-306.*

Chauhan, N.M. (2012). Impact and yield fissure inspection of gram through trainings and FLDs by KVK, Tapi in Gujarat.*Ind. J. of Agric. Res.* And Ext.Vol (4): 2011. PP: 12-15.

Chauhan, N.M. (2011). Execution of IPM Technology in Cotton Ecosystem of Tapi District. *Ind. J. of Agric. Res.* And Ext.Vol (4): 2011. PP: 31-34.

Chauhan, N.M. (2011). Livestock Management Practices followed by the dairy farmers of Narmada District of Gujarat. *Ind. J. of Agric. Res.* And Ext.Vol (4): 2011. PP: 67-70.

Chauhan, N.M. (2012).Contribution of the tribal farmwomen in livestock management. *Agric.Update*, vol.7 (1 and 2):5-7.

Chauhan, N.M. and Chauhan, N.B, (2012).Constraints faced and suggestions offered by the programme Coordinators of KKK's of India. *Agric. Update*, vol.7 (1 and 2):14-18.

Chauhan, N.M, (2010).Information Hungers of the rice growers. *Agric. Update*, vol.7 (1 and 2):72-75.

Chauhan, Nikulsinh M.(2012).Impact of Linkages with tribal cooperatives for effectual TOT inTribal belt. *Advance Research Journal of Social science* (An International refereed Research Journal). Volume-3, Issue (2), December-2012. PP: 227-230.

Pandya, C.D., G.R. Patel and N.M. Chauhan, (2012). Yield Gap Analysis of Okra Production Technology in Tapi District of South Gujarat *Agrobios Res.* Vol.1 (1), PP: 83-87(Jan-March-2012)

Chapter 11

Tribal Farmwomen in Agriculture and Dairy in Gujarat State

11.1 Abstract

Farmwomen are the backbone of Indian agriculture. Growing food has been an interminable saga of her life. Like other rural women, tribal farmwomen also play an important role in agriculture. No field operation is beyond the reach of women. They take important decisions in the home and outside the home Antoniades and Papayiannis. (2000). Keeping this fact in view the present investigation on role of tribal farmwomen in agriculture in Navsari district was undertaken with following objectives. (i) To study the participation of the tribal farmwomen in agriculture, animal husbandry and household activities along with correlations. (ii) To study the tribal farmwomen's involvement in decision making in Home, crop and animal husbandry.

Based on the study it was seen that Farmwomen's participation was seen highest in sowing, weeding and nipping/picking and threshing. The same was reported by Chauhan and Chauhan, (2009).In animal husbandry practices the frequency of participation of farmwomen was seen the highest in cutting and bringing a fodder followed. Chauhan, (2009) also reported the same. Farmwomen took a self-decision for decoration of house (79.17 per cent) and selection and preparation of food (70.83 per cent) in case of home management. Farm management was dominated by husband decision and majority of the farm management decision was taken by their husbands, animal husbandry management was completely dominated by women's self decision. The results are also in the line of Khanduri *et al.* (2004). The relationship between independent variables like age, education, herd size, land holding, family size and number of children of the respondents and their participation in crop husbandry was observed positively significant. Whereas the negative relationship was observed in case of occupation, type of family and age at marriage. Praveena *et al.* (2005) have reported the same results. The relation between independent variables of the respondents and their participation in animal husbandry was found negative for all of the independent variables except type of family only.

11.2 Introduction

Even cultural anthropological literature suggests that agriculture is invention of women. Farming in India is mainly a family occupation. Most of the family members are acutely engaged in farming. The farming capabilities for taking timely and judicious decisions by the farm families have a direct bearing on the agricultural development in country. There has been little realization about the contribution of women in the economic activities of a country. This was a position in most of counties till recently and India is no exception. The female population constitutes nearly half of the total population. It is a well recognized fact that more than 60 per cent of agricultural operations have been traditionally handled by women. In other area men are reluctant to share control with women. They also play a pivotal role in agriculture and livestock management. They still continued to share number of farm operations with men from early ages of invention of agriculture to the present day of modern agriculture.

Looking the significant role of tribal women in agriculture and allied activities, the study on rural woman's role in farm management was undertaken keeping in view of the increasing importance of involvement of rural women in agricultural production programmes. Studies in this field so far have exhibited a little concern on rural woman's role in Gujarat state. Hence, this study was conducted with an objective of ascertaining the role expectations and role performance of rural Tribal women in farm and livestock management.

11.3 Methodology of the Research

The present investigation was carried out in the Navsari district of the Gujarat state, which is one of the tribal districts of the state. In selecting the district the main consideration was the agriculture as the main occupation of people living in such villages. From the Navsari district, the six villages namely Adada, Aat, Chhapra, Hansapor, Matwad and Mogar were randomly selected for the study. From total selected 6 tribal dominated villages, 120 respondents were selected. Further, from the same list of tribal farm families, the tribal women who were decision makers and within the age group of 20-55 years were screened out. Finally by using random sampling technique, 20 respondents from each village were selected, thus a random sample of 120 respondents was selected for the study. The structured interview schedule keeping in view the objectives of the study was prepared in English. An interview schedule was used for the final data collection. Data were collected by arranging personal interview from the total selected 120 tribal farmwomen. As the study was concerned to find out the role performance of farmwomen in agriculture, ex-post-facto research design was used for this study. The statistical tools such as frequency, percent and correlation coefficient were used to interpret the data.

11.4 Result and Discussion

11.4.1.1 Participation of Tribal Farmwomen in Agriculture

1.1.1 Participation of Tribal Farmwomen in Pre-sowing and Sowing Operation

The perusal of the data in regards to participation of tribal farmwomen in pre-sowing and sowing operation revealed that the highest participation of tribal farmwomen was observed in sowing/transplanting followed by stubble collection, clod crushing, manuring and seedbed preparation/nursery. Chauhan and Thakor, (2006) also reported the same results.

11.4.1.2 Participation of the Tribal Farmwomen in Interculturing Operation

The data in regards to participation of tribal farmwomen in interculturing operation operations revealed that the highest participation of the tribal farmwomen was observed in weeding, followed by gap filling, application of fertilizer, bird scaring, irrigation, bunding and hoeing with hand, respectively. The same was reported by Chayal and Dhaka, (2010).

11.4.1.3 Participation of Tribal Farmwomen in Harvesting and Post-harvesting Operation

Perusal of the data in regards to participation of tribal farmwomen in harvesting and post-harvesting operation revealed indicated that the highest participation of the tribal farmwomen was observed in nipping/picking and threshing followed by harvesting, winnowing, storage, making threshing yard, bagging/packing and marketing of agricultural produce, respectively. The roles of tribal farmwomen in all the operations were observed up to the importance level. The similar trend was also reported by Chayal and Dhaka, (2010).

11.4.2 Participation of the Tribal Farmwomen in Animal Husbandry Practices

To understand real picture about tribal family, data were collected and results are presented in Table 13 and they are explained in following paragraphs.

The highest mean score of participation of tribal farmwomen was obtained in case of cutting and bringing a fodder Chauhan and Thakor, (2006). The next animal husbandry related operation performed by tribal farmwomen was compost making followed by watering and feeding to animals, milking, cleaning of cattle shed, selling of milk and its product, bathing of animals, preparation of milk products, grazing of animals, taking animal for bull and veterinary services. Chauhan, (2008) also reported the same. It can be concluded that the role of tribal farmwomen in most of the animal husbandry related operations were seen important. The possible reason for higher participation of women in animal husbandry would be that the most of the tribal farmwomen were possessing more than 2 animals. To increase family income tribal farmwomen might have taken keen interest in most of the animal husbandry related operations.

11.4.2.1 Involvementvements of the Tribal Farmwomen in the Process of Decision Making of Farm Management and Animal Husbandry

To determine the decision making pattern, the decision makers were categorized into four groups "Decision by herself", "Decision by her husband" "Joint decision by herself and any other member of her family including husband" "Decision not needed to take'. The similar result was also reported by Vijay Avinashilingam *et al.* (2010).

11.4.2.2 Tribal Farmwomen's Involvement in the Process of Decision Making about the Farm Management

Data collected from the respondents regarding their involvement in the process of decision-making about farm management are given in Table 1.

Table 1: Relationship between Independent Variable of the Respondents and their Participation in Crop Husbandry

n = 120

Sl.No.	*Independent Variables*	*Correlation Coefficient ('r' value)*
I.	**Personal variables**	
1.	Age	0.8430**
2.	Education	0.7409**
II.	**Economical variables**	
3.	Occupation	– 0.5553*
4.	Herd size	0.7854**
5.	Land holding	0.7774**
III.	**Social variables**	
6.	Family size	0.8074**
7.	Type of family	– 0.6284**
8.	Number of children	0.4918*
9.	Age of marriage	– 0.8709*

*: Significant at 5 per cent; **: Highly at significant at 1 per cent.

It is evident from the data that in majority of the decisions regarding farm management were husband dominated. Praveena *et al.* (2005). The joint decision made by tribal farmwomen and other members of family were hiring farm laborers (66.67 per cent), buying and selling of land (71.67 per cent) and selling of surplus farm produce (58.33 per cent), respectively. It can be concluded that the most of the farm decisions were made by husband of tribal farmwomen followed few decisions made jointly by the tribal farmwomen after discussion with any of their family members. It can be further concluded that tribal farmwomen had a recessive role in decision-making process regarding farm management.

11.4.2.3 Farmwomen's Involvement in the Process of Decision Making for Animal Husbandry

Perusal of the data presented in Table 2 concluded that the decision regarding animal husbandry was dominated by tribal farmwomen themselves as well as by joint decision with family members. The husband remained recessive in decision making about animal husbandry. Majority of the farmwomen were taking self-decision regarding fodder and marketing of milk and milk products. The joint decisions taken were selection of animal breed, sale and purchasing of animal as well keeping size of herd, some of the decisions were not needed to take by them because some of them had no animal or some of them were not selling milk and its products. The same was reported by Chauhan, (2008).

Table 2: Relationship between Independent Variable of the Respondents and their Participation in Animal Husbandry

n = 120

Sl.No.	*Independent Variables*	*Correlation Coefficient ('r' value)*
I.	**Personal variables**	
1.	Age	– 0.8888*
2.	Education	– 0.8411*
II.	**Economical variables**	
3.	Occupation	– 0.3014*
4.	Herd size	– 0.9464*
5.	Land holding	– 0.8881*
III.	**Social variables**	
6.	Family size	– 0.9322*
7.	Type of family	+ 0.8646*
8.	Number of children	– 0.8036*
9.	Age of marriage	– 0.8709*

*: Significant at 5 per cent.

11.4.3 The Relationship between Selected Independent Variables and Crop and Animal Husbandry

Out of nine independent variables only three variable *viz* occupation, Type of family and age at marriage were found negative where as Six variables like- age, education, herd size, land holding, family size and number of children were observed positively and significantly with their participation in crop husbandry practices. The similar results were also reported by Chauhan, (2009).

11.3.4 Independent Variables of the Respondents and their Participation in Animal Husbandry

Data presented in Table 2 indicated that out of nine independent variables only type of the family found significant with their participation in animal husbandry. Remaining all of the independent variables had negative and significant relationship with their participation in animal husbandry. Bisht *et al.* (2000) reported the results on this line.

11.5 Summary and Conclusion

In this portion of the research paper the findings of the study have been given in a nutshell.

11.5.1 Participation of Tribal Farmwomen in Agriculture and Animal Husbandry

The highest participation of tribal farmwomen was seen in sowing/transplanting followed by stubble collection, clod crushing, manuring and seedbed preparation/ nursery management. The highest participation of the tribal farmwomen was observed in weeding followed by gap filling, application of fertilizer, bird scaring, irrigation, bunding and hoeing with hand, respectively. The highest participation of the respondents were in nipping/picking and threshing followed by harvesting, winnowing, storage, making threshing yard, bagging/packing and marketing of agricultural produce, respectively. The highest mean score of participation of tribal farmwomen was obtained in case of cutting and bringing a fodder. Other participation of tribal farmwomen was seen in compost making followed by watering and feeding to animal, milking, cleaning of cattle shed, selling of milk and its products, bathing of animals, preparation of milk products, grazing of animals, taking animal for bull and veterinary services.

11.5.2 Involvement of the Tribal Farmwomen in Decision-Making

The majority of the decisions regarding farm management were not performed by tribal farmwomen, thus they were husband dominated decisions such as, when to irrigate the fields (87.50 per cent), quantity and type of fertilizers to be used in the farm (85.00 per cent) introduction of new crop variety, buying farm machinery/ equipment, using plant protection measures, borrowing money for farm operation, installing oil engine, electric motor and pumps, selection of seed, deciding area to be sown under each crop etc. The joint decision was made only in case of hiring farm laborers (66.67 per cent), buying and selling of land and selling of surplus farm produce. It can be concluded that the tribal farmwomen did not play dominant role in making important decisions of farm management. The decisions about selection of fodder and feed was dominated by tribal farmwomen (81.67 per cent) followed by sale of milk and its products. The jointly taken decisions were sale and purchase of animals (65.00 per cent) followed by selection of animal breed and keeping size of herd. It can be concluded that the important decisions regarding animal husbandry were dominated by tribal farmwomen themselves. The husbands remain recessive in decision-making regarding animal husbandry. Chauhan and Thakor R, (2006) reported the same.

11.5.3 Correlation Study of Crop Husbandry

The positive significant relationship was seen between the role of tribal farmwomen in crop husbandry and their age, education, herd size, land holding, family size and number of children. Whereas, the negative relationship was observed among occupation, type of family, age at marriage and their role in crop husbandry. The relationship between all independent variables and the role of tribal farmwomen was observed negative except type of family.

11.6 Conclusion

Based on the study it was seen that Farmwomen's participation was seen highest in sowing, weeding and nipping/picking and threshing. The same was reported by Chauhan and Chauhan, (2009).In animal husbandry practices the frequency of participation of farmwomen was seen the highest in cutting and bringing a fodder followed. Chauhan, (2009) also reported the same. Farmwomen took a self-decision for decoration of house (79.17 per cent) and selection and preparation of food (70.83 per cent) in case of home management. Farm management was dominated by husband decision and majority of the farm management decision was taken by their husbands, animal husbandry management was completely dominated by women's self decision. The results are also in the line of Khanduri *et al.* (2004). The relationship between independent variables like age, education, herd size, land holding, family size and number of children of the respondents and their participation in crop husbandry was observed positively significant. Whereas the negative relationship was observed in case of occupation, type of family and age at marriage. Praveena *et al.* (2005) have reported the same results. The relation between independent variables of the respondents and their participation in animal husbandry was found negative for all of the independent variables except type of family only.

11.7 Implication of the Study

Some important implications emerging from the findings of the study are presented below.

1. It was seen that many agricultural, animal husbandry related and house hold activities were performed by the tribal women, but when questions comes to take decisions regarding all these matter, their roles were seen skimpy. As tribal farmwomen are the key units of the family of the tribal's' community and they have skill in talking good decisions regarding all economic activities of the family, their participation in decision talking process needs to be encouraged by those people who are involved in the development of tribal.
2. Special measures need to be taken to increase the enrolments of girls in schools and to impart non-formal education for the dropouts, so that they would be able to keep accounts and made wage distribution to labors.
3. There is need to strengthen informal tribal education programme as means to the develop farm and home by providing modern agricultural technologies. The tribal farmwomen should be given training for another productive work outside the home especially for marginal and small size of holding. The family planning programme should be made more popular in this area.
4. The opportunities for productive employment should be enhanced by establishing agro-based industries, which might be organized in form of co-operatives. The tribal farmwomen should be allowed to take active part in decision-making process. These decisions will be more rational and practical oriented.

Eye Opening Points for Policy Makers

Recommendations

1. The roles performed by the rural women in home, crop and livestock administration and the factors affecting to them are of paramount importance to the planners, decision makers, researchers, educationist, governments, NGOs, farming communities and extension workers occupied in the process of rural development.
2. Prime importance in decision making regarding home, crop and live stock management should be given to tribal farmwomen for betterment of rural tribes in general and farming occupation as a whole.
3. More milk co-operatives should be started in Tribal areas and the management should be handed over to tribal farmwomen for superior development of dairy industries and farming occupation as a in one piece.
4. The government should establish a community internet centre (**CICs**) at village level to satisfy the knowledge hunger of tribes and decorate them to fight in open global market.
5. More emphasis should be given to create an able tribal women resource for sustainable agricultural growth.
6. Tribal women should be the target groups for next phase of green revolution on sustainable base.

References

Antoniades, A. and Papayiannis, C, (2000). The role of women in the family farm of the mountain region of Cyprus. Agricultural-Economics-Report, Cyprus Agricultural Research Institute, Nicosia, 39, pp. 12.

Bisht, B. S.; Bhuchar, S. K.; Pushpa, Pant; Kothyari, B. P.; Palni, L.M.S.; Pant, P; Allen, R. (ed.); Schreier, H. (ed.); Brown, S. (ed.); Shah, P. B. (2000). The pivotal role of women in the hills: gender analysis in Arah village in Uttar Pradesh, central Himalayas, India. Proceedings of a workshop held in Baoshan, Yunnan Province, China, March 2-5 1999, pp. 35-46.

Chayal, K and Dhaka, B.L. (2010). Analysis of Role Performance of Women in Farm activities. *Indian Res. J. Ext. Edu.*10 (2):109-112.

Chauhan,N.M. (2008). Livelihood of Tribal Farmwomen through Livestock Management, Paper presented in *International Seminar* on Strategies for Livelihood Security of Rural poor at ICAR Research complex, Ila, old Goa, during 24th-27th September-2008.pp-164, organized by International Society of Fxtension education, Nagpur, MS.

Chauhan,N.M. (2012). Involvement of Tribal Farmwomen in Decision making.*Indian Research Journal of Extension Education*. Special Issue, (Volume-II), 2012. PP: 172-174.

Chauhan,N.M. (2009). Crop Husbandry with Participation of Tribal farmwomen.Paper presented in on "Participatory Approach in rural Development" on 31st August at JAU, Junagadh, Guajarat.

Chauhan,N.M. (2009). Participation of Tribal farmwomen in Animal Husbandry Paper presented in seminar on "Participatory Approach in rural Development" on 31st[st] August-2009 at JAU, Junagadh, Guajarat.

Chauhan, N.M. and Chauhan, N.B. (2012).Participation of tribal farmwomen in agriculture and dairy. Paper published in *GAU. Res. J.* Vol-38(2), july-2013, page no. 106-111.

Chauhan, N.M. and Thakor, R.F. (2006). Participation of tribal farmwomen in Agriculture. A paper presented in *National seminar* on "Rural Development through People's Participation", held at Marathawada Agricultural University (MAU), Parbhani, Maharashtra, during 27-28th February-2006 organized by Indian Society of Extension education.

Chauhan, N.M. and Thakor, R,(2006).Participation of the Tribal farmwomen in Decision making published in *Gujarat Journal of Extension Education*, Anand,Vol.XVI-XVII, December,2005-2006, pp-55-57.

Khanduri, B. K.; Rukma, R. and Rawat, R. (2004). Role of women in sustaining life in Garhwal Himalaya, Uttaranchal. Economic-Affairs-Calcutta. 48(3): 152-161.

Praveena,P.L.R.J., M. AchutaRama Rao and P. Venktata Rao(2005). Decision making pattern of rural women in farm related activities. *Agril. Ext. Review*. 17. (6): 3-5.

Vijay Avinashilingam, N.A. Upayana Singh and Ramkumar. (2010).Role performance of Kota Tribal Households in Dairying. *Indian Res. J. Ext. Edu.*10 (2):104-108.

Chapter 12

Self-Reliance in Paddy Seed through Seed Village Programme-Success Story

12.1 Abstract

Krishi Vigyan Kendra Vyara is located in the Tapi district – the southeastern part and the tribal belt of Gujarat. Small and Marginal farmers are often at a disadvantageous position in absorbing the agricultural technology related to genetic enhancement of production potential of agricultural crops. This is because of centralized production and distribution of improved seeds by a seed companies. Though the organized sector is able to produce a large quantity of seeds, the supply chain is unable to cope with the huge demand for seeds across the length and breadth of the country. Thus, the farming community depends to a large extent on external sources for important inputs such as seeds. Seed village programme provide an alternative to this problem and help farmers become self reliant. This initiative needs both organized communities and scientific backstopping. Efforts towards up scaling seed village programme under Krishi Vigyan Kendra, Vyara in the Tapi district resulted in encouraging learning outcomes and demonstrated the viability of seed village with suitable technical backstopping by KVK scientist and empowerment of the community members. The seed village concept not only ensure good quality seeds for enhancing productivity but also in generating income for the community members resulting in improved livelihood. The self sufficiency in the seed is a great impact in the area like Tribal dominated District of Tapi. Implication of this study is the whole stocks of the seed materials have been sold by high remunerative rates at farmer's field only. The consciousness of the farmers regarding quality seed materials have been increased drastically. The cheating and looting by private seed traders have been reduced remarkably and the area under recommended cultivars of paddy has been developed in clusters and it leads towards value addition through need based paddy production for industrial use as well as for food grain purpose. The seed village concept of the farmers have been cultivated in the mind of orthodox tribal farmers to shift their age old seed through recently released high yielding paddy varieties. It was really a big achievement in the field of agriculture to run on sustainability and profitability super high way.

12.2 Introduction

Krishi Vigyan Kendra Vyara is located in the Tapi district – the southeastern part and the tribal belt of Gujarat. The district shares it borders with Surat, Navsari and Dang district in North-west, South and East respectively with Maharashtra state in East.The geographical area of the district is 7.79 lack ha. The conspicuous features of the district are undulating topography with steep slopes and heavy rainfall. The av. Rainfall of the district is about 80 –100 inches per annum. The distribution is erratic and thus, causing damage to the crops likes Pulses, Paddy and other cereals. The district is composed largely of tribal communities. This, communities depend primarily on agriculture for their livelihood supplemented by income from seasonal employment in nearest industrial town. Soils of the district in general can be classified as medium black to heavy black, Red Murom and rocky with low innate fertility. Agriculturally, about 60 per cent of the cultivated area is undersigned crop during monsoon. The main crops of the district are – Paddy, Sorghum, Groundnut, Pulses, Sugarcane, Gram and vegetables-Brinjal, Okra. Paddy is the staple foods of the tribal communities of the district. Among Vegetable crops Okra is main crop for export quality.

Krishi Vigyan Kendra

KVK Vyara is working under the auspices of Navsari Agricultural University. It has started its activities since September, 2000. Kendra has undertaken **Seed multiplication programme of Paddy since 2000-01**.

12.3 Genesis of Programme

To ascertain the constraints encountered by Paddy growers of this area, a Benchmark survey was carried out by multidisciplinary team of scientist of KVK during the year 2009-10. The results of the survey revealed following …

a. Large majority of the tribal farmers are cultivating conventional varieties (Tichun native –1, Sathi and Kada) of paddy.

b. Conventional varieties are early mature, having coarse grain with dull husk colour, and highly susceptible to water logging as the rain coincide with maturity of paddy in later stage.

c. Paddy growers are using higher seed rate *i.e.* 30 – 40 Kg for transplanting 1 acre of land as they produce seed of their own.

d. They were planting 10-12 seedlings/hill resulting in to over plant population and lower yield. It also increases the cost of cultivation because harvesting takes much time.

e. Farmers were using impure seed, as they produce it on their farm without taking much care.

f. Av. Yield of Paddy (conventional varieties) is about 2500 Kg./ha under good management practices.

g. Market value of the conventional varieties is less ranges between Rs. 5–6/ Kg. because of coarse grain and unpleasant colour of husk.

h. Tribal farmers are not satisfied with yield status of conventional varieties of Paddy.

i. The farmers having assured irrigation facilities or low land kyari expressed their desired to have high yielding variety with **late maturity** to avoid damage by rains to crop at the maturity time.

j. On the contrary, farmers growing paddy under rainfed condition expressed their desire to have high yielding **early mature** variety.

k. It was also noticed that most of the tribal farmers posses small piece of land. Whatever they produced from the land during monsoon, they have to depend on it for their livelihood. They are striving hard for their food especially during August and September.

The basic concept of seed village is to make the villagers self-sufficient for quality sees of their region. The seeds produced of the appropriate varieties of various crops, locally. The following steps may be taken to ensure effective implementation of seed village programme.

1. As far as possible, seed village should be organized in a compact area with adequate irrigation facilities comprising of few adjacent villages.
2. The area selected for seed village should produce enough seeds to meet the requirement of the particular area (*i.e.*) block or district for which seed village has been organized.
3. The area entitled for seed village programme may not be changed every year but it should be kept permanent for 5-10 years.
4. The selected farmers should be provided with training in seed production so that they are in a position to take all possible care for quality seed production.
5. Adequate quantity of source seeds should be mobilized in advance
6. Adequate inputs should be made available in time
7. Integrated plant protection measures should be advocated.
8. Seed processing facilities should be made available at the nearest destination
9. Proper planning should be made to distribute the seeds produced in time.
10. The seed producers may attempt for successful implementation of seed village concept in their areas. It is always better to test the seeds or seed lots

before sowing or offering for sale. To test the seeds a service sample should be drawn and submitted to the Seed Testing Laboratory. Following should be born in while drawing a service sample.

11. Prescribed quantity of seed samples should be sent along with the sample slip
12. In the sample slip the details on crop, variety, lot number should be indicated clearly.
13. A fee of Rs.20 per sample should be paid for each service sample
14. If the moisture test is required a separate sample should be sent in a polythene container with 70 gauge thickness
15. A regular training programme was conducted to the seed law enforcement officials on 15.6.2010 at KVK Vyara about 50 officials participated in this training programme.
16. The Subject Matter Specialist of Krishi Vigyan Kendra, Vyara inspected Paddy seed production field in Tapi district on 28-9-2010 and guided the seed grower for successful seed production.

12.4 Seed Growing through Woman Cooperative

Seed is an important determinant of agricultural production and the efficacy of other agricultural inputs like labour, fertilizers depends on the quality of seed. Hence, the availability of the right seed material is very crucial. In Tapi district Paddy is grown in an area of 114291 ha and the approximate seed requirement is around 6857t. In order to achieve higher seed requirement, a major effort is required to cover more area under seed production. The production and supply of quality seeds and enhancing the seed replacement rates of various crops are the important issues in seed sector. Hence, training on seed production to the farmers is needed to increase the production of quality seeds.

Krishi Vigyan Kendra Intervention

The farmers have purchased the seeds from private seed companies, government outlets and also used their own farm saved seeds. KVK scientists explained the uses and production of quality seeds. But, the resource poor farmers were unable to produce the seeds of their own due to lack of technical know- how. Then the Krishi Vigyan Kendra intervened and trained the farmers of Hangati Mahila trust, Mandal about the seed production technologies such as land selection, sources of seed, isolation distance, rouging, foliar nutrition, harvesting and post harvest handling of seeds in three stages under seed village training programme

If we consider the success story of trained farmers of Hangati Mahila Trust villages in Tapi District is one of the progressive farmers in this village has shown impressive progress both as an early adopter and entrepreneur. He is also a convener and SAC member of Krishi Vigyan Kendra, Vyara.

12.5 KVK Intervention

Two days training programme on **'Seed Production Technology'** was imparted to the farmers on the basic aspects of Seed Production technology, improved technologies on Integrated nutrient Management etc., were given at Krishi Vigyan Kendra, Vyara and field exposure visit was arranged in the Seed Village Scheme fields at Vyara so as to acquire practical skill on the production technology. The farmers were supplied with resource materials on seed production Technology.

The farmers had acquired modern technologies and skill. A very good impact has been created among the farmers and in turn they developed confidence in the seed production. The farmer prepared nursery his land by ploughing followed by rotavator and finally prepared his nursery bed for paddy seedlings. He applied farm yard manure @ 15-20 t/ha during ploughing and incorporated in the land.

Paddy seeds of Jaya and Gurjari, treated with thirum @ 3 gm/kg were sown in the second week of June 2010 with the suitable guidelines of the scientists. Irrigation and fertilizer were given in nursery after 23rd days after sowing transplanting of Paddy was done with line planting recommended spacing, fertilizer and irrigation according to the prescribed schedule given by the scientists of KVK.

By the seed production technology, he could achieve uniform crop stand, limited weed problem and problems of pest and diseases. He has harvested the Paddy crop during the third week of October 2010. He obtained yield of 6.5 t/ha.

A field day was conducted in the field of Hangati Mahila Trust farmers of Zarali, Jamkhadi, Bharadada, Amalgundi etc villages so as to create awareness among the other farmers on the achievement of higher yield in Paddy by Seed Production technology. Most of the farmers had expressed the advantages of raising Paddy for getting higher returns within a period of four months It is imperative that seed production technology has to be scaled up over larger area in forthcoming years, thereby the farmers fetch higher yield and higher net return. In such attempts, the role of KVK is very vital and necessary.

Table 1: Seed Village Trainings to the Farmers

Sl.No.	*Activity*	*No.*	*Participants*
1.	On/Off campus training programme	17	270
2.	Field days	4	578

Table 2: Impact of the Trainings

Sl.No.	*Particulars and Impact of the Training*	*Production and Income Details*
1.	Area	30 Acre
2.	Crops in which seed produced	Paddy, Pulse
3.	Unit production capacity	6.5 tones/ha –Paddy
4.	Seed supply	Krishi Vigyan Kendra, Vyara
5.	Net income	Rs.64,000/ha –paddy
6.	Rural employment	2500 man days/year
7.	Estimated area coverage	25 ha.–paddy

12.6 Impact

He is having 30 acres of wet land with good irrigation sources. Previously, he followed conventional system of rice cultivation for grain production. After few years he felt that this system would not have benefit in terms of both yield and soil fertility maintenance. Then, he planned to start seed production in rice as advised by scientists of Krishi Vigyan Kendra, Vyara. Previously he had undergone the training on the direct seeding techniques with drum seeder and SRI techniques in rice during 2009. He practiced these techniques in seed production and he found that this techniques required low seed rate (2-3 kg ha^{-1}), nitrogen (LCC based nitrogen management), water and labour requirement. Based on this experience, he extended to an area of 30 acres for seed production in rice. He was able to harvest higher seed yield of 6400 kg ha^{-1} with low cost of cultivation (Rs.12,500/ha) when compared with conventional method. Now he became an Own Hangati Mahila trust seed entrepreneur and marketing his seeds by this trust in their jurisdiction of Tapi District.

12.7 Summary

Small and Marginal farmers are often at a disadvantageous position in absorbing the agricultural technology related to genetic enhancement of production potential of agricultural crops. This is because of centralized production and distribution of improved seeds by a seed companies. Though the organized sector is able to produce a large quantity of seeds, the supply chain is unable to cope with the huge demand for seeds across the length and breadth of the country. Thus, the farming community depends to a large extent on external sources for important inputs such as seeds. Seed village programme provide an alternative to this problem and help farmers become self reliant. This initiative needs both organized communities and scientific backstopping. Efforts towards up scaling seed village programme under Krishi Vigyan Kendra, Vyara in the Tapi district resulted in encouraging learning outcomes and demonstrated the viability of seed village with suitable technical backstopping by KVK scientist and empowerment of the community members. The seed village concept not only ensure good quality seeds for enhancing productivity but also in generating income for the community members resulting in improved livelihood. The self sufficiency in the seed is a great impact in the area like Tribal dominated District of Tapi.

12.8 Implication

The whole stocks of the seed materials have been sold by high remunerative rates at farmer's field only. The consciousness of the farmers regarding quality seed materials have been increased drastically. The cheating and looting by private seed traders have been reduced remarkably and the area under recommended cultivars of paddy has been developed in clusters and it leads towards value addition through need based paddy production for industrial use as well as for food grain purpose. The seed village concept of the farmers have been cultivated in the mind of orthodox tribal farmers to shift their age old seed through recently released high yielding paddy varieties. It was really a big achievement in the field of agriculture to run on sustainability and profitability super high way.

Chapter 13

Impact and Yield Fissure Inspection of Gram through Training and FLDs by KVK, Tapi

13.1 Abstract

To uphold rural development programmes, the ability of farmers should be increased through systematic training so that they may understand each constituent of the recommended technologies. In Tapi district farmers were obtaining very low yield in Gram. Low productivity of gram was due to lack of knowledge about scientific cultivation, land configuration, poor nutrient management and lack of knowledge in IPDM. The gram cultivation is highly profitable in tribal dominated areas of the Surat and Tapi district. This crop is also advisable to the farmers for upgrading of the soil physical, chemical and biological health. The human health point of view this crop is highly advisable to the people of the tribal region to control the diseases related to the mal nutrition and deficit syndromes. The study was undertaken in Tapi district of South Gujarat. Results regarding overall knowledge of gram indicated that the low, medium and high level of knowledge before contact with KVK was 78.00 per cent, 16.00 per cent and 06.00 per cent, respectively and it was improved up to 08.00 per cent, 10.00 per cent and 82.00 per cent after contact with KVK (Table 1).

Results of Knowledge regarding selected scientific innovations for gram reflected high knowledge regarding selected scientific innovations were found *viz* 87.00 per cent regarding new high yielding varieties, 83.00 per cent for integrated nutrient management, 81.00 per cent Land configuration and 78.00 per cent Seed rate, respectively, (Table2). The perusal of data presented Table 3 indicated that majority of the farmer had low level of knowledge (76.00 per cent) before contact with KVK.

After contact with KVK, 84.00 per cent of the farmers had high level of knowledge. Data present in table 4 indicated that 89.00 per cent of the farmer had adopted new high yielding variety fallowed by land configuration (85.00 per cent), INM (83.00 per cent), seed rate (82.00per cent) and so on. From the above discussion, it could be inferred that after imparting training and other intensive approach by KVK, Tapi, majority (82.00 per cent) of the tribal farmers of these area had high the knowledge level and majority (84.00 per cent) of the tribal farmers of these area had high adoption level about package of practices of gram crop. At the end we can suggest this crop in the region is an important for increasing the income, improving the soil health, fertility and productivity and also to raise the standard of living of the tribes. The technology index indicates the feasibility of evolved technology at the farmer's field. Lower the value of technology index, more is the feasibility of the technology demonstrated, (Sagar and Chandra, 2004). As such reduction of technology index from 48.92 per cent (2008-09) to 45.00 per cent (2010-11) exhibited the feasibility of technology demonstrated.

13.2 Introduction

A number of agricultural improvement programmes have been introduced in India to increase the agricultural production and income of the farming communities. But the outcomes of these programmes are not satisfactory in terms of achieving higher agricultural production. The most important factor responsible for this poor outcome was lack of understanding of various technological recommendations by the farmers (P.K. Singh, 2002). Recognizing the importance of technical recommendation as necessary condition for rural development, more emphasis on farmers training activities has been placed in different Five year plans. It is now widely accepted fact that training to farmers increases the technical and allocative efficiencies with the farming business as a whole. Tribal area of Tapi district grow gram on moisture conserve or in light irrigation, but they get very low yield due to use of low yielding variety, poor knowledge about scientific cultivation of gram. KVK, Tapi had done intensive effort on training about scientific cultivation, demonstration on new variety and land configuration Kushare and Sahane. (2011). KVK conducted 7 on campus and 7 off campus trainings, total number of beneficiaries of FLD is 112 covering 20 villages of Tapi district and other extension activities during last three year. To find out the impact and yield gap of the same this study was conducted in Tapi District. The objectives of the study were (1) To know the Overall knowledge of scientific package of practices of Gram. (2) To study the Knowledge regarding selected scientific innovations for Gram cultivation (3) To study the Overall adoption of scientific package of practices of Gram. (4) To know the extent of adoption of scientific practices of Gram cultivation (per cent). (5) To find out the yield gap analysis of gram production technology.

13.3 Methodology

Five villages were selected purposively for the study. Among each village 20 farmers were selected randomly. So, total sample size was 100 tribal farmers. The data were collected through personal interview. The interview schedule was prepared by keeping the objectives of the study in mind. The necessary care was taken to collect the unbiased and correct data. The data were collected, tabulated and analyzed to find out the findings and drawing the conclusion. The statistical tools like frequency and percentage were employed to analyze the data. The extension gap, technology gap and the technology index were worked out with the help of formulas given by the Samui *et al.* (2005) as mentioned below:

Extension gap = Demonstration yield- Farmers yield

$$\text{Technology index} = \frac{(\text{Potential yield} - \text{Demonstration yield}) \times 100}{\text{Potential yield}}$$

13.4 Results and Discussion

Table 1: Overall Knowledge of Package of Practices of Gram Crop

n=100

Category	*Before Contact with KVK (per cent)*	*After Contact with KVK (per cent)*
Low level of knowledge	78	08
Medium level of knowledge	16	10
High level of knowledge	06	82

Data depicted in table 1 indicated that 78.00 per cent of the farmers had low level of knowledge which was increased (82.00 per cent) after contact with KVK. D. Uma *et al.* (2010) also reported the same.

Table 2: Knowledge Regarding Selected Scientific Innovations for Gram Crop

n=100

Sl.No.	*Selected Scientific Innovation*	*Low*	*Medium*	*High*
1.	New high yielding varieties	08	05	87
2.	Land configuration	06	13	81
3.	Seed rate	14	08	78
4.	Bio fertilizer	19	06	75
5.	Weeding	17	12	71
6.	Integrated Nutrient management	07	10	83

Data show in the Table 2 indicated that 87.00 per cent of the farmers had knowledge about new high yielding varieties followed by Integrated Nutrient management (83.00 per cent), Land configuration (81.00 per cent) and bio fertilizer (75.00 per cent). Dr. Mamoni Das *et al.* (2010) reported the same results.

Data presented in Table 3 indicated that 76.00 per cent of the farmers had low level of adoption which was increased after contact with KVK (84.00 per cent). Bhagwan Singh and Chauhan, (2010) also reported the same.

Table 3: Overall Adoption of Scientific Cultivation of Gram (Percentage)

n=100

Category	*Before Contact with KVK (per cent)*	*After Contact with KVK (per cent)*
Low level of adoption	76	04
Medium level of adoption	18	12
High level of adoption	06	84

Table 4: Adoption of Critical Gram Production Technology (per cent)

n=100

Sl.No.	*Name of Technology*	*Adoption (per cent)*
1	New high yielding varieties	89
2	Land configuration	85
3	Seed rate	82
4	Bio fertilizer	78
5	Weeding	72
6	Integrated Nutrient management	76

The data show in the Table 4 indicated that 89.00 per cent of the farmers had new high yielding varieties which were followed by Land configuration (85.00 per cent), Seed rate (82.00 per cent) and Bio fertilizer (78.00 per cent). Meena and Dheeraj Singh. (2011) reported the same in case of cumin.

From the above discussion, it could be said that overall knowledge level and adoption level of the tribal farmers about package of practices of gram had increased up to 82.00 per cent and 84.00 per cent, respectively after imparting training by KVK, Tapi. Singh, P. K. 2002 had also reported the same.

1. Yield Gap Analysis of Gram Cultivation

The results obtained during three years are presented in Table 6. The results indicated that the highest yield in FLD plots and farmer's plots was 22.32 qt and 13.75 qt per hectare respectively. The yield of gram under demonstration ranged between 17.46 qt to 21.10 qt/ha over observation period. The results clearly showed that due to knowledge and adoption of scientific practices, the yield of gram could be increased by 36.72 per cent,45.78 per cent and 46.19 per cent over the yield obtained under farmers practices. The above findings are in line with the findings of Singh (2002), Dubey *et al.* (2010) and Dr. B.S. Meena, (2010).Average extension gap was 5.74 quintal per hactare, which emphasized the need to train the farmers through various extension resources like trainings and FLDs. The technology gap was ranged between 11.25 qt/ha and 12.23 qt/ha. The average technology gap minimized during three years of FLD programme was 11.66 qt/ha. The technology gap observed may be attributed dissimilarity in the soil fertility status, agricultural practices and local climate conditions. The technology index indicates the feasibility of evolved technology at the farmer's field. Lower the value of technology index, more is the feasibility of the technology demonstrated, (Sagar and Chandra, 2004). As such reduction of technology index from 48.92 per cent (2008-09) to 45.00 per cent (2010-11) exhibited the feasibility of technology demonstrated. The FLD obtained a significant positive result and also provided the researchers an opportunity to demonstrate the productivity potential and profitability of the integrated nutrient management under real farm situation, which they have been advocating for a long time. Similar findings were reported by Kirar *et al*. (2005). (Table 6)

Table 5: Particular Showing the details of Okra Growing under FLD and existing practices

Particulars	*Demonstration Practices*	*Farmer's Practices*
Variety	GG-2	Deshi Variety
Fertilizer	Bio-compost – 6 ton/ha	Basal – None
	Chemical Fertilizer – 20 + 40 + 00	Chemical Fertilizer-not used
Seed treatment	*PSB* and *Rhizobium* – 2 lit/2 kg/ha	—NIL—

13.5 Conclusion

From the above discussion, it can be concluded that knowledge level and adoption level of the tribal farmers were amplified after imparting training and conducting FLDs by KVK scientists. KVK, Vyara is working as a knowledge hub for latest agricultural technology in Tapi district. The Front Line Demonstration conducted on Integrated Nutrient Management in gram at farmer's fields in Tapi district of Gujarat revealed that the farmers could increase gram production significantly. In demonstration the Integrated Nutrient Management of gram performed better than control plots. It improves the productivity by 42.90 per cent. The productivity gain under FLD over farmer's practice created awareness and motivated the other farmers to adopt Integrated Nutrient Management and high yielding varieties of gram in the district.

13.6 Implication

This study sheltered the way for extension workers for effective and efficient TOT in the field of Agricultural Extension.The heartfelt efforts made by extension workers would always be resulted in good impact and feedback. The technology index indicates the feasibility of evolved technology at the farmer's field. Lower the value of technology index more is the feasibility of the technology demonstrated.This study suggest for conducting intensive trainings, FLDs and effective use of all means of extension education to educate the gram growers for higher production of gram and to get higher net return on sustainable basis.

Table 6: Exploitable Productivity, Extension Gap, Technology Gap and Technology Index of Gram as Grown Under FLD's and Existing Package of Practices

Year	*Area*	*No. of Demo.*	*Yield q ha^{-1}*			*FP*	*Per cent Increase in Yield Over FP*	*Extension Gap q ha^{-1}*	*Technology Gap q ha^{-1}*	*Technology Index*
			Highest	*Lowest*	*Average*					
2008-09	5	39	18.78	16.10	17.46	12.77	36.72	4.69	12.23	48.92
2009-10	5	39	20.34	18.37	19.68	13.50	45.78	6.18	11.50	46.00
2010-11	5	34	22.32	19.53	20.10	13.75	46.19	6.35	11.25	45.00
Mean			20.48	18.00	19.08	13.34	42.90	5.74	11.66	46.64

References

Bhagwan Singh and T.R. Chauhan, (2010).Adoption of Mungbean Production Technology in Arid Zone of Rajasthan. *Indian Res. J. Ext.Edu.*10 (2):73-77

Chauhan, N.M. (2012).Impact and Yield crack analysis of trainings and FLDs regarding scientific practices of gram.*Agriculture Update*, Volume-7(Issue 3 and 4) August and November-2012.pp:199-202.

Chauhan, N.M. (2012). Knowledge level of Farmers Regarding Package of Practices for Gram Crop. *Journal of Krishi Vigyan*, July-December-2012, Vol-1, Issue-1(2012), Page No- 46-48.

D. Uma Maheswara Rao, Dr, P. Chandrashekara and Dr. R. Veeraiah,(2010).Impact of Training Programmes of Krishi Vigyan Kendra, *Agricultural Extension Review*, January-March, Vol.1(1):1-3

Dr. B.S. Meena, (2010).Socio-Economic characteristics and Technology use pattern of Farmers. *Agricultural Extension Review*, January-March, Vol.1(2):16-17

Dr. Mamoni Das, Dr. N.N. Puzari and Dr. B.K. Ray, (2010).Impact of Training of Skill and Knowledge Development of Rural Women. *Agricultural Extension Review*, January-March, Vol.1(1):29-30

Dubey, Swapnil, Tripathy Sarvesh, Singh Pradyuman and Sharma Rakesh Kumar, 2010. Yield gap analysis of black gram production through frontline demonstration. *J. of Progressive Agriculture*. 1(1): 42-44

Kirar, B.S., Mahajan, S. K., Nshine, R., Awasthi, H. K. and Shukla, R. N., 2005. Impact of technological practices on the productivity of Soybean in Frontline demonstration. *Ind. Res. J. of Ext. Edu.* 5(1): 15-17

Kushare, B.M. and Sahane, U.G. (2011).front Line demonstration- An effective tool for increasing productivity of nizer in Thane district of Maharashtra. *Int. J. Agri. Sci.Vol-7(2):249-253.*

N.M. Kale and Priti M. Todasam. (2010).Utility perception of Soybean Growers about Recommended Cultivation Technologies. *Agricultural Extension Review*, January-March, Vol.1(2):7-8

Meena, M.L. and Dheeraj Singh.(2011). Impact of Front Line Demonstration in Adoption of Improved Cumin Production Technology.*Int. J. Ext. Edu.* Vol-7, PP: 24-28

Sagar, R. L. and Ganesh Chandra, 2004. Front line demonstration on sesame in West Bengal. *Agricultural Extension Review*. 16(2): 7-10

Samui, S. K. Maitra, S., Roy, D. K., Mandal, A. K., Saha, D. 2000. Evaluation of front line demonstration on groundnut. *J. of the Indian Society Costal Agricultural Research*. 18(2): 180-183

Singh, P. K. 2002. Impact of participation in planning on adoption of new technology through FLD. MANAGE *Extension Research Review*. July-Dec: 45-48

Chapter 14

Impact and Yield Gap Analysis of Trainings and FLDs Regarding Scientific Practices of Okra Cultivation

14.1 Abstract

KVK, Tapi has started an integrated campaign for okra cultivation on scientific line. KVK, Tapi conducted numbers of Front Line Demonstrations (FLDs) on farmer's field. In addition to this, KVK, Vyara has also imparted On/Off campus trainings and other extension activities during last three years in 7 villages of Tapi district under RKVY project. Very few efforts have been made by the behavioral scientists to know the responses of farmers about the scientific practices of okra cultivation for its sustainability and augmentation in its production and productivity, Kirar, B.S., *et al.*, 2005. The Front Line Demonstrations are conducted under the close supervision of KVK scientists for transfer of technology (TOT). The basic purpose of these demonstrations is to test research findings on farmer's field and to get direct feedback from the farmers so, the researchers can reorient their research and training programmes. Keeping in this view, the present study was carried out to know the collision of these demonstrations with following objectives: To find out the level of knowledge of farmers about scientific practices of okra cultivation, to know the extent of adoption of scientific practices of okra cultivation and to find out the yield gap analysis of okra production technology. Results revealed that the significant improvement in knowledge and adoption of scientific cultivation of okra was seen in beneficiaries. Also significant decrease was seen in the value of technology index. From the above discussion, it can be concluded that knowledge level and adoption level of the tribal farmers were amplified after imparting training and conducting FLDs by KVK scientists. KVK, Vyara is working as a knowledge hub for latest agricultural technology in Tapi district. The Front Line Demonstration conducted on Integrated Nutrient Management in okra at farmer's fields in Tapi district of Gujarat revealed that the farmers could increase okra production significantly. In demonstration the Integrated Nutrient Management of okra performed better than control plots. It improves the productivity by 45.06 per cent. The productivity gain under FLD over farmer's practice created awareness and motivated the other farmers to adopt Integrated Nutrient Management in okra in the district.

14.2 Introduction

The Okra crop is becoming more and more popular in Tapi district of Gujarat State. In this District the sizeable acreage area (4000 hectare) is under okra cultivation. Due to lack of knowledge regarding scientific package of practices tribal farmers are assassinating huge budget behind crop production, indiscriminating use of agrochemicals and loosing the health of soil, water and environment and in addition to that they are unable to get higher net return.Owing to lack of knowledge regarding value addition, Post Harvest Management (PHT) and market management they are unable to get higher recompenses from okra farming Jogender Singh and Rahul, (2010). To overcome this problem KVK, Tapi has started an integrated campaign. KVK, Tapi conducted numbers of Front Line Demonstrations (FLDs) on farmer's field. In addition to this, KVK, Vyara has also imparted On/Off campus trainings and other extension activities during last three years in 7 villages of Tapi district under RKVY project. Very few efforts have been made by the behavioral scientists to know the responses of farmers about the scientific practices of okra cultivation for its sustainability and augmentation in its production and productivity, Kirar, B.S., *et al.*, 2005. The Front Line Demonstrations are conducted under the close supervision of KVK scientists for transfer of technology (TOT). The basic purpose of these demonstrations is to test research findings on farmer's field and to get direct feedback from the farmers so, the researchers can reorient their research and training programmes. Keeping in this view, the present study was carried out to know the collision of these demonstrations with following objectives:

1. To find out the level of knowledge of farmers about scientific practices of okra cultivation.
2. To know the extent of adoption of scientific practices of okra cultivation.
3. To find out the yield gap analysis of okra production technology.

14.3 Materials and Methods

The present study was conducted purposively in seven selected FLD villages of Vyara and Songadh talukas of RKVY project running under KVK in Tapi district in Gujarat State during the year 2007-08 to 2009-10. In these villages, on/off campus training programmes and other extension activities were carried out during these years. Three adopted villages were also selected randomly from the Vyara and Songadh Talukas in which mandatory activities of KVK were carried out. From each village, 10 farmers growing okra were selected randomly making sample size of 100. The data were collected through personal interview with the help of teacher's made scale. The score was given accordingly. The statistics like frequency, mean and standard deviation were worked out and interpretation was done in light of objectives. For yield gap analysis, KVK Vyara conducted demonstrations in FLD villages of RKVY project during the period 2007-08 to 2009-10. A total of 24 farmers were covered under this programme. The demonstration of Integrated Nutrient Management was taken in area of 0.25 ha was covered in 3 years. To compare with FLDs, a control plot was maintained at each location. Customary visit by the KVK scientists to the demonstration fields were made to guide the farmers. The critical inputs like hybrid variety, bio-compost, PSB and Azotobacter were supplied to the farmers by the KVK. The yield data were collected from both the FLD plots and control plots and their extension gap, technology gap and the technology index were worked out with the help of formulas given by the Samui *et al.* (2005) as mentioned below:

Extension gap = Demonstration yield- Farmers yield

$$\text{Technology index} = \frac{(\text{Potential yield} - \text{Demonstration yield}) \times 100}{\text{Potential yield}}$$

14.4 Results and Discussion

14.2.1 Knowledge of Scientific Practices of Okra Cultivation

Results of overall knowledge of scientific practices of okra cultivation indicated that the medium and high level of knowledge before KVK intervention was 35.00 per cent and 10.00 per cent, respectively. This was increased to the tune of 56.00 per cent and 28.00 per cent after contact with of KVK (Table 1).

Table 1: Overall Knowledge Kevel of Scientific Practices of Okra Cultivation

n=100

Category	*Before Contact with KVK (per cent)*	*After Contact with KVK (per cent)*
Low level of knowledge	55	16
Medium level of knowledge	35	56
High level of knowledge	10	28

Knowledge regarding scientific practices of okra cultivation was observed medium and high level knowledge which was 35.00 per cent and 39.00 per cent,respectively with respect to integrated nutrient management (INM), Where as in integrated pest management (IPM) it was seen 61.00 per cent and 14.00 per cent,respectively. Higher knowledge level regarding plant growth regulators and value addition was recorded 82.00 per cent and 78.00 per cent, respectively (Table 2).it is really an admired effort made by the KVK Scientists. Dr. Mamoni Das *et al.* (2010) reported the same.

Table 2: Knowledge Regarding Scientific Practices of Okra Cultivation

n=100

Sl.No.	Selected Scientific Innovation	Low	Medium	High
1.	New high yielding varieties	16	28	56
2.	Seed rate	11	16	73
3.	Integrated Nutrient management	26	35	39
4.	Integrated Pest Management	25	61	14
5.	Knowledge regarding yellow mosaic virus/powdery mildew	26	43	31
6.	Plant growth regulator	7	11	82
7.	Value addition	6	16	78

14.2.2 Adoption of Scientific Practices of Okra Cultivation

The data presented in Table 3 indicated that medium and high level of adoption 69.00 per cent and 17.00 was seen before KVK intervention. Whereas it was 28.00 per cent and 68.00 per cent respectively after conducting the demonstration by KVK. Bhagwan Singh and Chauhan, (2010) reported the same results.

Table 3: Overall Adoption of Scientific Practices of Okra Cultivation

n=100

Category	Before Contact with KVK (per cent)	After Contact with KVK (per cent)
Low extent of adoption	14	4
Medium extent of adoption	69	28
High extent of adoption	17	68

Adoption of okra production technology, 82.00 per cent farmers adopted high yielding varieties and INM. 76.00 per cent farmers adopted recommended seed rate. In case of plant growth regulator and value adoption 73 per cent.00 per cent and 77.00 per cent adoption was observed (Table 4). It may be due to constant follow up by KVK scientist and live contact with farmers maintained by KVK team. **D. Uma** ***et al.*** (2010) also reported the same.

14.2.3 Yield Gap Analysis of Okra Cultivation

The results obtained during three years are presented in Table 6. The results indicated that the highest yield in FLD plots and farmer's plots was 161.70 qt and 112.50 qt per hectare, respectively. The yield of okra under demonstration ranged between 143.07 qt to 156.11 qt/ha over observation period. The results clearly showed that due to knowledge and adoption of scientific practices, the yield of okra could be increased by 41.37 per cent, 43.73 per cent and 50.06 per cent over the yield obtained under farmers practices. The above findings are in line with the findings of Singh (2002), Dubey *et al.* (2010) and Dr. B.S. Meena, (2010). Average extension gap was

Table 4: Adoption of Scientific Practices of Okra Cultivation

n=100

Sl.No.	*Name of Technology*	*Adoption (per cent)*
1.	New high yielding varieties	82
2.	Seed rate	76
3.	Integrated Nutrient management	82
4.	Integrated Pest Management	61
5.	Knowledge regarding yellow mosaic virus/powdery mildew	72
6.	Plant growth regulator	73
7.	Value addition	77

47.72 q ha$^{-1,}$ which emphasized the need to educate the farmers through various extension means like FLD. The technology gap was ranged between 18.30 qt/ha and 36.93 qt/ha. The average technology gap less than three years FLD programme was 26.37 qt/ha. The technology gap observed may be attributed dissimilarity in the soil fertility status, agricultural practices and local climate conditions. The technology index indicates the feasibility of evolved technology at the farmer's field. Lower the value of technology index, more is the feasibility of the technology demonstrated, (Sagar and Chandra, 2004). As such reduction of technology index from 20.51 per cent (2007-08) to 10.17 per cent (2009-10) exhibited the feasibility of technology demonstrated. The FLD obtained a significant positive result and also provided the researchers an opportunity to demonstrate the productivity potential and profitability of the integrated nutrient management under real farm situation, which they have been advocating for a long time. Similar findings were reported by Kirar *et al*. (2005). (Table 6)

Table 5: Particular Showing the details of Okra Growing Under FLD and Existing Oractices

Particulars	*Demonstration Practices*	*Farmer's Practices*
Variety	Hybrid	Hybrid
Fertilizer	Bio-compost – 5 ton/ha	Basal – None
	Chemical Fertilizer – 150 + 50 + 50	After 21 day – 100 kg A.S. and 60 kg DAP
		After one month – 80 kg A.S. up to crop mature
Seed treatment	PSB and Azotobacter – 1 lit/8-10 kg seed	—NIL—

14.3 Conclusion

From the above discussion, it can be concluded that knowledge level and adoption level of the tribal farmers were amplified after imparting training and conducting FLDs by KVK scientists. KVK, Vyara is working as a knowledge hub for

Table 6: Exploitable Productivity, Extension Gap, Technology Gap and Technology Index of Gram as Grown Under FLD's and Existing Package of Practices

Year	*Area*	*No. of Demo.*	*Yield q ha^{-1}*			*FP*	*Per cent Increase in Yield Over FP*	*Extension Gap q ha^{-1}*	*Technology Gap q ha^{-1}*	*Technology Index*
			Highest	*Lowest*	*Average*					
2007-08	2	8	160.03	105.06	143.07	101.20	41.37	41.87	36.93	20.51
2008-09	2	8	167.80	153.80	161.70	112.50	43.73	49.20	18.30	10.17
2009-10	2	8	162.40	104.03	156.11	104.03	50.06	52.08	23.89	13.27
Mean	2	8	163.41	120.96	153.63	105.91	45.06	47.72	26.37	14.65

latest agricultural technology in Tapi district. The Front Line Demonstration conducted on Integrated Nutrient Management in okra at farmer's fields in Tapi district of Gujarat revealed that the farmers could increase okra production significantly. In demonstration the Integrated Nutrient Management of okra performed better than control plots. It improves the productivity by 45.06 per cent. The productivity gain under FLD over farmer's practice created awareness and motivated the other farmers to adopt Integrated Nutrient Management in okra in the district.

14.4 Implication

This study paved the way for extension workers for effective and efficient TOt in the field of Agricultural Extension.The heartfelt efforts made by extension workers would always be resulted in good impact and feedback. The technology index indicates the feasibility of evolved technology at the farmer's field. Lower the value of technology index more is the feasibility of the technology demonstrated.This study suggest for conducting intensive trainings, FLDs and effective use of all means of extension education to educate the okra growers for production of export oriented okra and to get higher net return on sustainable basis.

References

Bhagwan Singh and T.R. Chauhan, (2010).Adoption of Mungbean Production Technology in Arid Zone of Rajasthan. *Indian Res. J. Ext.Edu.*10 (2):73-77

Chauhan, N.M.(2012).Knowledge and Adoption of Scientific practices of okra cultivation in tapi District.*Green Farming (An International Journal)*, Vol.3 (6) 2012, PP: 659-760.

D. Uma Maheswara Rao, Dr, P. Chandrashekara and Dr. R. Veeraiah,(2010).Impact of Training Programmes of Krishi Vigyan Kendra, *Agricultural Extension Review*, January-March, Vol.1(1):1-3

Dr. B.S. Meena, (2010).Socio-Economic characteristics and Technology use pattern of Farmers. *Agricultural Extension Review*, January-March, Vol.1(2):16-17

Dr. Mamoni Das, Dr. N.N. Puzari and Dr. B.K. Ray, (2010).Impact of Training of Skill and Knowledge Development of Rural Women. *Agricultural Extension Review*, January-March, Vol.1(1):29-30

Dubey, Swapnil, Tripathy Sarvesh, Singh Pradyuman and Sharma Rakesh Kumar, 2010. Yield gap analysis of black gram production through frontline demonstration. *J. of Progressive Agriculture*. 1(1): 42-44

Kirar, B.S., Mahajan, S. K., Nshine, R., Awasthi, H. K. and Shukla, R. N., 2005. Impact of technological practices on the productivity of Soybean in Frontline demonstration. *Ind. Res. J. of Ext. Edu.* 5(1): 15-17

Kushare, B.M. and Sahane, U.G. (2011).front Line demonstration- An effective tool for increasing productivity of nizer in Thane district of Maharashtra. *Int. J. Agri. Sci.Vol-7(2):249-253.*

N.M. Kale and Priti M. Todasam. (2010). Utility perception of Soybean Growers about Recommended Cultivation Technologies. *Agricultural Extension Review*, January-March, Vol.1(2):7-8

Meena, M.L. and Dheeraj Singh.(2011). Impact of Front Line Demonstration in Adoption of Improved Cumin Production Technology.*Int. J. Ext. Edu.* Vol-7, PP: 24-28

Sagar, R. L. and Ganesh Chandra, 2004. Front line demonstration on sesame in West Bengal. *Agricultural Extension Review.* 16(2): 7-10

Samui, S. K. Maitra, S., Roy, D. K., Mandal, A. K., Saha, D. 2000. Evaluation of front line demonstration on groundnut. *J. of the Indian Society Costal Agricultural Research.* 18(2): 180-183

Singh, P. K. 2002. Impact of participation in planning on adoption of new technology through FLD. MANAGE *Extension Research Review.* July-Dec: 45-48

Chapter 15
Impact of Training Regarding Package of Practices of Soybean Crop

15.1 Abstract

A number of agricultural development programmes have been introduced in India to increase the agricultural production and income of the farming communities. But the outcomes of these programmes are not satisfactory in terms of achieving higher agricultural production. The most important factor responsible for this poor outcome was lack of understanding of various technological recommendations by the farmers. G.L. Kothari *et al.* (2006). Recognizing the importance of technical recommendation as necessary condition for rural development, more emphasis on farmers training activities has been placed in different Five year plans. It is now widely accepted fact that training to farmers increases the technical and allocative efficiencies with the farming business as a whole. To support rural development programmes, the ability of farmers should be increased through systematic training so that they may understand each component of the recommended technologies. In Tapi district farmers were obtaining very low yield in Soybean. Low productivity of Soybean was due to lack of knowledge about scientific cultivation, poor nutrient management and lack of knowledge in IPDM. The soybean cultivation is highly profitable in tribal dominated areas of the Surat and Tapi district. This crop is also advisable to the farmers for improvement of the soil physical, chemical and biological health. The human health point of view this crop is highly advisable to the people of the tribal region to control the diseases related to the mal nutrition and deficiency syndromes. Farmers of Tapi district growing rainfed drill paddy but its produce very low yield so it's get very low remunerative. In place of drill paddy soybean crop earn more net profit then drill paddy. KVK conducted 8 on campus and 10 off campus trainings, total number of beneficiaries of FLD is 43 covering 7 villages of Tapi district and other extension activities during last three year. Total number of beneficiaries of FLD is 97 covering 7 villages of Tapi district and other extension activities during last three year. Impact study results are presented here. To find out the impact of the same this study was conducted in Tapi District. The objectives of the study were (1) To know the Overall knowledge of scientific package of practices of Soybean. (2) To study the Knowledge regarding selected scientific innovations for Soybean cultivation (3) To study the Overall adoption of scientific package of practices of Soybean. (4) To find out the Adoption of critical Soybean production technology (per cent). The results seen Results of overall knowledge of soybean indicated that the low, medium and high level of knowledge before contact with KVK was 89.00 per cent, 09.00 per cent and 02.00 per cent, respectively and it was increased up to 07.00 per cent, 14.00 per cent and 79.00 per cent after contact with KVK (Table 1).

In case of Knowledge regarding selected scientific innovations for soybean high knowledge regarding selected scientific innovations were found except seed rate (Table2). The perusal of data presented Table 3 indicated that Data presented in table -3 indicated that majority of the farmer had low level of knowledge (75.00 per cent) before contact with KVK. After contact with KVK, 89.00 per cent of the farmers had high level of knowledge. Data present in table 4 indicated that 92.00 per cent of the farmer had adopted new high yielding variety fallowed by INM (88.00 per cent).From the above discussion, it could be inferred that after imparting training and other intensive approach by KVK, Tapi, majority (79.00 per cent) of the tribal farmers of these area had high the knowledge level and majority (89.00 per cent) of the tribal farmers of these area had high adoption level about package of practices of soybean crop. At the end we can suggest this crop in the region is an important for increasing the income, improving the soil health, fertility and productivity and also to raise the standard of living of the tribes.

15.2 Methodology

Five villages were selected purposively for the study. Among each village 25 farmers were selected randomly. So, total sample size was 100 tribal farmers. The data were collected through personal interview. The interview schedule was prepared by keeping the objectives of the study in mind. The necessary care was taken to collect the un- biased and correct data. The data were collected, tabulated and analyzed to find out the findings and drawing the conclusion. The statistical tools like frequency and percentage were employed to analyze the data.

15.3 Results and discussion

Results of overall knowledge of soybean indicated that the low, medium and high level of knowledge before contact with KVK was 89.00 per cent, 09.00 per cent and 02.00 per cent, respectively and it was increased up to 07.00 per cent, 14.00 per cent and 79.00 per cent after contact with KVK (Table 1).

Table 1: Overall Knowledge of Package of Practices of Soybean Crop

n=100

Category	Before Contact with KVK (per cent)	After Contact with KVK (per cent)
Low level of knowledge	89	07
Medium level of knowledge	09	14
High level of knowledge	02	79

Table 2: Knowledge Regarding Selected Scientific Innovations for Soybean Crop

n=100

Sl.No.	Selected Scientific Innovation	Low	Medium	High
1.	New high yielding varieties	10	5	85
2.	Seed rate	13	74	13
3.	Bio fertilizer	11	16	73
4.	Weeding	23	8	69
5.	Integrated Nutrient management	09	13	78

In case of Knowledge regarding selected scientific innovations for soybean high knowledge regarding selected scientific innovations were found except seed rat.

Table 3: Overall Adoption of Scientific Cultivation of Soybean (Percentage)

n=100

Category	Before Contact with KVK (per cent)	After Contact with KVK (per cent)
Low level of adoption	75	05
Medium level of adoption	13	06
High level of adoption	12	89

Data presented in Table 3 indicated that majority of the farmer had low level of knowledge (75.00 per cent) before contact with KVK. After contact with KVK, 89.00 per cent of the farmers had high level of knowledge.

Table 4: Adoption of Critical SPybean production Technology (per cent)

n=100

Sl.No.	Name of Technology	Adoption (per cent)
1.	New high yielding varieties	92
2.	Seed rate	87
3.	Bio fertilizer	73
4.	Weeding	70
5.	Integrated Nutrient management	88

Data present in Table 4 indicated that 92.00 per cent of the farmer had adopted new high yielding variety fallowed by INM (88.00 per cent).

From the above discussion, it could be inferred that after imparting training and other intensive approach by KVK, Tapi, majority (79.00 per cent) of the tribal farmers of these area had high the knowledge level and majority (89.00 per cent) of the tribal farmers of these area had high adoption level about package of practices of soybean crop. At the end we can suggest this crop in the region to increase the income of the farmers and also to improve their own, family as well as soil health.

The study has acknowledged the knowledge level of the farmers towards profitable cultivation of the soybean. This study can be guideline for other extension worker to implement this way of extension technology for their clients in their respective area of operation for TOT. On this foundation the extension personnel may locate clients for training and also those who can be used as counselors to other farmers. The study is also useful for effective propagation of the new technology in other regions for eco friendly and sustainable agricultural development. The study also reflects the role of KVKs in effective Transfer of Technologies (**TOTs**) at grass root level.

15.4 Conclusion

From the above discussion, it can be concluded that the impact of training conducted by KVK has beneficial effect on knowledge level and adoption level of the tribal farmers about scientific cultivation of Soybean. Nirmal Kumar *et al.* (2005) reported the same. Results of overall knowledge of soybean indicated that the low, medium and high level of knowledge before contact with KVK was 89.00 per cent, 09.00 per cent and 02.00 per cent, respectively and it was increased up to 07.00 per cent, 14.00 per cent and 79.00 per cent after contact with KVK (Table 1). In case of Knowledge regarding selected scientific innovations for soybean high knowledge regarding selected scientific innovations were found except seed rat. Data presented in table -3 indicated that majority of the farmer had low level of knowledge (75.00 per cent) before contact with KVK. Results reported by Kokate and Kharde, (2006) were also in same line. After contact with KVK, 89.00 per cent of the farmers had high level of knowledge. Data present in table 4 indicated that 92.00 per cent of the farmer had adopted new high yielding variety fallowed by INM (88.00 per cent).

15.5 Implications

The high-tech trainings on Soybean production and marketing technologies has changed the vision of the tribal farmers. New motor cycles had been purchased by tribal youths only due to higher income through Soybean. Five Tribal farmers were able to purchase four wheelers from scientific Soybean cultivation. The whole pockets became famous for profit oriented Soybean cultivation. The NRIs originated from this district can say in foreign countries that this Soybean is coming from my native. In real sense this success has changed the vision of the KVK scientists towards farming communities and vice versa. This KVK has proved the real role of Information hub in the tribal dominated areas like, Tapi district. This can be a model for other extension workers and all related with rural development.

References

Chauhan, Nikulsinh M. (2012). Impact of Training Regarding Package of Practices of Soybean Growers. *Guj. J. Extn. Edu.* XX-XXI, 2007-2008, PP: 39-40.

G.L. Kothari, S.L Intodia and F.L. Sharma (2006). Extent of Knowledge and Adoption of Maize production Technology by the Farmers of Agro-climatic ZoneIV Rajasthan. Asian J. of Ext. Edu, 25:23-27

J. Tulsiram and Ravi M. Sambrani (2006). A study on Adoption Pattern of Farmers in Different Drought Areas. *Asian J. of Ext. Edu*, 25:28-31.

K.D. Kokate and P.B. Kharde, (2006), Extension Strategies for increasing Sugarcane production.Asian J. of Ext. Edu, 25:10-14.

Nirmal Kumar, S.K. Rautary, M. Gupta and A.K. Singh(2005).Impact of Summer School n Mechanization f Rice Production System. Indian J. of Ext. Edu, 41:54-57.

S. Das, S.N. Laharia and V.B. Dixit.(2005). Impact of Leadership Style on Job Satisfaction. Indian J. of Ext. Edu, 41:12-19.

S.R. Meena and Anita Jhamtani (2005).Change in Cropping Pattern Subsequent to Farm Mechanization. Indian J. of Ext. Edu, 41:31-36.

Chapter 16

Impact of IPM Mechanism and Constrains of Cucurbitaceous Vegetable Growers

16.1 Abstract

IPM is such a technology that reduces the cost of plant protection and increase the yield. It also helps in reducing the pesticide use and thus, prevents/delays development of pesticide resistance, reduces residues in soil, water, food and definite role in the prevention of environment imbalance. The mechanical control of pest is very cheaper and feasible for farmers to adopt the same. The study was conducted in Tapi district of South Gujarat. The district has serious problems of fruit fly in Cucurbitaceous family vegetables. The Cue lure for fruit fly was proved very effective control measures for fruit fly. The reduction in fruit fly infestation was 80.70 per cent. Reduce in number of sprays were 80.00 per cent. Yield increased up to 15.84 t/ ha.Income of the farmer was increased 13540 Rs./ha. Expenditure behind fruit fly control was decreased to the tune of Rs. 1450 per hectare and Net income of farmers was increased to the tune of Rs. 14990 per hectare. The overall knowledge in respect to Knowledge about insect pests of crop, Knowledge about fruit fly and its damage, Knowledge about fruit fly trap and Knowledge about integrated management of fruit fly was increased after intervention of KVK. The constraints in adoption of the technology were categorized based on opinions got from respondents.

16.2 Introduction

Vyara Taluka of Tapi district is situated at the border of Gujarat and Maharashtra. It is located 70 km from Surat and it is Krishi Vigyan Kendra headquarter. The Vyara block of Tapi district is famous for vegetable cultivation and it is also exporting vegetables in huge amount. It is the tribal dominated district having 84 per cent population belongs to tribal community. Cucurbitaceous vegetables *viz.*, bitter gourd, small gourds, cucumber etc. are infested by two species of fruit flies *i.e.* melon fruit fly, *Bactocera cucurbitae* (Coquilleti) and the Ethiopian fruit fly, *Dacus ciliatus* (Loew), which limits the economic returns to the farmers by their damage to the final product *i.e.*, fruits. The female fly insert its eggs in soft tender fruit tissue by piercing fruits with the ovipositor, as a result, a watery fluid oozes from the punctures which on hardening become resinous brown. The maggots emerged from the eggs, start feeding on pulp of the fruit. The secondary infection by microorganisms from site of egg laying cause rotting of the fruits rendered them unfit for the consumption. This reduces the market value of the produce. The infested fruits become distorted and drop. The mature maggots jumped out of the fruits and pupate inside the soil. The extent of loss reported to be varied from 30 to 100 per cent depending upon cucurbits species and the season. As the maggot being an internal feeder, it is rather difficult to control the maggot. The only option is to manage the adult fruit flies and that too before they mat and female deposit eggs. The chemicals means *i.e.* using insecticides for managing fruit flies is no longer effective. The melon fruit fly, *B. cucurbitae* can be effectively managed by Male Annihilation Technique by attracting large numbers of males through "Cue Lure", a pheromone of *B. cucurbitae*. But, the other species of fruit fly *i.e.*, *D. ciliatus* cannot be managed by Male Annihilation Technique as no pheromones/Para pheromones are available. To manage this species, application of insecticides with baiting technique is useful. Therefore, to administer both the species integrate approach using field sanitation, large scale destruction of males by Male Annihilation Technique and application of insecticidal baits is effective. Recently, Navsari Agricultural University has developed a specialized NAUROJI trap using cue lure. In this trap a ply wood blocks of size 5cm x 5 cm x 1 cm impregnate with cue lure are used. To popularize the integrated management technique as well as the trap developed by the university, front line demonstrations were given to the farmers of Khadaka chikhali village of Vyara taluka, Dist. Tapi during the year 2007-08 and 2008-09.The interested farmers were given training with special emphasis on fruit fly species, their life cycle, nature of damage, and management strategies through power point presentations. To know the adoption of the cue lure it is essential to conduct the impact study of the same.

16.3 Materials and Methods

The study was conducted in Khadka Chikhali village of Tapi District in the state of Gujarat. From each faliya (**Pargana**) 10 farmers were selected randomly for the study. The total sample size was 100.For selection of the respondent the list of cucurbitaceous vegetable growers was collected with the help of field workers, VLWs and resource persons. The selected respondents were personally interviewed with the help of specially designed interview schedule. The data were subjected to exploratory statistical analysis. The frequency, per cent and constraints were employed to interpret the data and drawing conclusion. The study was under taken to measure the impact of Cue lures in cucurbetacea vegetable. The detailed components of IPM were (1). Regular collection of damaged and fallen fruits and destruction with deep burying or by burning.(2)Installation of "Cue Lure" NAUROJI traps @10 per hectare and (3) Application of bait using fermented water with jaggery and insecticide endosulfan applied as large droplets with broom are demonstrated, constant follow up visits were made and field days were organized.

16.4 Results and Discussion

The experimental findings are discussed underneath.

1. Knowledge of Fruit Fly Control in Farmers of the Village

Knowledge Level

The attempt was made to know the Knowledge of fruit fly control in farmers of the village in the form of different components and presented in Table 1. The overall knowledge in respect to knowledge about insect pests of crop, knowledge about fruit fly and its damage, knowledge about fruit fly trap and knowledge about integrated management of fruit fly was increased after intervention of KVK; same was also confirmed by Narkar *et al.* (2004).

Table 1: Knowledge of Fruit Fly Control in Farmers of the Village

n=100

Sl.No.	*Particulars*	*Before FLD*	*After FLD*
1	Knowledge about insect pests of crop	Low	High
2.	Knowledge about fruit fly and its damage	Low	High
3.	Knowledge about fruit fly trap	Nil	High
4.	Knowledge about integrated management of fruit fly	Nil	High

2. Adoption of Recommended Package of Practices of IPM

Adoption Level

The overall adoption of IPM technology in cotton was studied and quoted in Table 2.It is palpable from Table 2 that majority of the cotton growers about recommended IPM practices of cotton growers(57.00 per cent) had medium level of adoption of IPM components. There were 16.00 per cent and 27.00 per cent of the respondents had low and high level of adoption in general, respectively; same was also confirmed by Narkar *et al.* (2004).

Table 2: Distribution of the Creeples Growers as per Over all Adoption of IPM Aids

n=100

Sl.No.	*Category*	*Frequency*	*Per cent*
1.	Low Adoption	39	16.00
2.	Medium Adoption	81	57.00
3.	High Adoption	30	27.00

3. Crop Parameters from which Impact Gain Measured

Table 3: Crop parameters from which impact gain measured

Sl.No.	*Particulars*	*Year*	*Treated*	*Untreated*	*Per cent Increase/ Reduction*
1.	Per cent infestation	2007-08	4.8 (3-6 per cent)	18.75 (12-40 per cent)	87.00
		2008-09	2.95 (0-6 per cent)	23.55 (10-40 per cent)	74.40
		Average	3.879	21.15	**80.70**
2.	Reduce in number of sprays	2007-08	1	5	80
		2008-09	1	5	80
	Average	1	5	**80.00**	
3.	Yield t/ha	2007-08	10.54	9.62	9.56
		2008-09	10.19	8.31	22.12
	Average	10.365	8.965	**15.84**	
4.	Income of the farmer Rs./ha.	2007-08	94860	86580	8280
		2008-09	101900	83100	18800
		Average	98380	84840	**13540**
5.	Expenditure/ha.	2007-08	1050	2500	1450
		2008-09	1050	2500	1450
		Average	1050	2500	**1450**
6.	Net income of farmers	2007-08	93810	84080	9730
		2008-09	100850	80600	20250
		Average	97330	82340	**14990**

The study was also included to know the Crop parameters from which impact gain measured and depicted in Table3.The data presented in table3 revealed that The Cue lure for fruit fly was proved very effective control measures for fruit fly. The reduction in fruit fly invasion was 80.70 per cent. Reduced in number of sprays were 80.00 per cent. Yield increased up to 15.84 t/ha.Income of the farmer was increased 13540 Rs./ha. Expenditure behind fruit fly control was decreased to the tune of Rs 1450 per hectare and Net income of farmers was increased to the tune of Rs. 14990 per hectare. Rombade *et al.* (2011) also reported the same results. The results are also in conformity to Moradia, (2011).

4. Distribution of the Vegetable Grower Respondents as per their Constraints in Adoption of Biocontrol

Data presented in Table4 revealed that the constraints faced by vegetable growers to adopt cue lure in their cucurbetacea were Lack of knowledge about *Cue lure,* Lack of knowledge about installing *Cue lure,* Lack of knowledge about *benefits of Cue lure,*

Monetary problems, *Cue lure* not available in market, No sprays of chemical due to loss of other beneficial insect-pests and lack of effective extension help. The constraints were categorized as per perception of the vegetable growers and presented in Table 4.

Table 4: Distribution of the Vegetable Grower Respondents as per their Constraints in Adoption of Biocontrol

n=100

Sl.No.	*Constraints in Adoption*	*Frequency (150)*	*Per cent*
1.	Lack of knowledge about *Cue lure*	136	91.00
2.	Lack of knowledge about installing *Cue lure*	40	27.00
3.	Lack of knowledge about *benefits of Cue lure*	105	70.00
4.	Monetary problems	95	63.00
5.	*Cue lure* not available in market	85	57.00
6.	No sprays of chemical due to loss of other beneficial insect-pests.	92	61.00
7.	Lack of effective extension help	35	23.00

5. Extension Activities Carried Out in the Village Khadka Chikhali

The total extension activities carried out in the same village by KVK Tapi was also deliberated and depicted in Table 5.The constant follow up, live contact and multifarious extension activities carried out by KVK scientists were reflected in impact study.

Table 5: Extension Activities Carried Out in the Village Khadka Chikhali

Sl.No.	*Name of Activity*	*No.*	*Beneficiaries*
1	Training :On campus: Off campus	FiveTwo	12087
2.	Visits to farmers	Eleven	97
3.	Field day cum impact study	One	129
4.	Impact study conducted	One	100
5.	Follow up visits of KVK Scientists	Eleven	56

16.5 Conclusion

IPM is such a technology that reduces the cost of plant protection and increase the yield. It also helps in reducing the pesticide use and thus, prevents/delays development of pesticide resistance, reduces residues in soil, water, food and definite role in the prevention of environment imbalance. The mechanical control of pest is very cheaper and feasible for farmers to adopt the same. The study was conducted in Tapi district of South Gujarat. The district has seviour problems of fruit fly in Cucurbitaceous family vegetables. The Cue lure for fruit fly was proved very effective control measures for fruit fly. The reduction in fruit fly infestation was 80.70 per cent. Reduce in number of sprays were 80.00 per cent. Yield increased up to 15.84 t/ ha.Income of the farmer was increased 13540 Rs./ha. Expenditure behind fruit fly control was decreased to the tune of Rs 1450 per hectare and Net income of farmers was increased to the tune of Rs. 14990 per hectare. The overall knowledge in respect to Knowledge about insect pests of crop,

Knowledge about fruit fly and its damage, Knowledge about fruit fly trap and Knowledge about integrated management of fruit fly was increased after intervention of KVK. This may be due to the proper guidance given by KVK scientists, Demonstrations and constant follow up by KVK missionary. The cue lure was found most suitable control measures among fruit flies in creeples.

16.6 Implication

The study has acknowledged the knowledge level of the vegetable growers towards IPM technology. This study can be guideline for other extension worker to implement this way of extension technology for their clients on IPM.On this foundation the extension personnel may locate clients for training and also those who can be used as counselors to other farmers. The study is also useful for effective propagation of the IPM technology in other regions for eco friendly and sustainable agricultural development. The constraints faced by vegetable growers in adoption of Biocontrol would be useful to extension workers, governments and all related to agriculture and rural development.

This study will be a guideline for other extension workers to perform better in their field. It leads toward effective, efficient and result oriented work in the field of Agricultural extension. This is a mile stone work for the effective TOT in the Tribal dominated interior region of the south Gujarat. It will be eye opening for disseminating any recently released innovative agricultural technology successfully among illiterate and poor participants. At the outset of the concluding we can say KVK Vyara is becoming really an **information hub** for farming communities. Our efforts are to make this KVK Farmers friendly, farmers centric, farmers leading and the overall agricultural development on sustainable basis. Precision farming and Eco friendly development of the region is our prime Motto. The **Research-Extension-Farmer-Market** Linkage Extension approach is a current need of the time to get better agricultural output. The **next phase of Green Revolution** can only be possible through integration of all above said approaches.

16.7 References

A.M. Moradia. (2011).Effect of Trichoderma species on Macrophomina phaseolina. *Internat. J. agric. Sci.*, 7(2) (June, 2011), PP: 458-459.

Ankulwar, B.N., Jondhale, S.G. and Rangari, P.V.(2001). Extent of adoption of recommended package of practices of sunflower in far. *Maharashtra. J. Ext. Edu.*20:63-65.

Bokade, H.D., Gaikwad, S.P. and Kalantri, L.B. (2009). Study of adoption lelvel of bio-fertilizers by the farmers.Agric. Update. 4(1 and 2): 211-213.

Chauhan, N.M. (2012). Effect of IPM Component on cucurbitaceous vegetables. *Rashtriy Krishi.*, Volume.7 (1), June -2012 Page No- 12-13.

Chauhan, N.M. (2012). Espousal and Constraints in Adoption of IPM Technologies in Cotton Ecosystem in Tapi District.Paper presented in Attended the *National level Seminar* on "India Cotton: Gearing up for Global Leadership "at Main Cotton research Station, NAU, Surat during 6-8th January-2013.Organized by NAU, Indian and Society of Cotton Improvement, Mumbai.Seminar Compendium page No:78.

Godase, S.S. (2002). Adoption of bio-control measures for cotton by the farmers. M.Sc. Thesis, P.G. Institute. Dr. PDKV, Akola, M.S.(India).

Gaikwad, S.P., Godase, S.S., Tambe, B.N. and Dhane, A.S. (2011). Study of constraints faced by cotton growers in adoption of bio-control measures. *Internat. J. agric. Sci.*, 7(2) (June, 2011), PP: 306-308.

Pandey, Rakesh, Chaudhary, R.P., Chaturvedi, A.K. and T.N. Rai. (2011).Level of knowledge and scientific orientation towards integratwed pest management among vegetable growers. *Internat. J. agric. Sci.*, 7(2) (June, 2011), PP: 396-399.

T.G. Ugale, Vrushali, L. Bedse and N.R. Toke. (2011).Integrated management of gram pod borer, *Helicoverpa armigera* (Hubner). *Internat. J. agric. Sci.*, 7(**2**) (June, 2011), PP: 333-335.

Chapter 17

Appraisal of Training Needs of Members of Tribal Women SHGs for Agriculture Management

17.1 Abstract

The study of 100 members of the Tribal Women SHGs from Sinnar taluka of Nashik district revealed that the members in general are not conscious in full of the SHG concepts and latest crop production and marketing technology. The study further revealed that 81 per cent of the respondents suggested providing information on SHG concepts and linkage programme. Seventy-nine per cent suggested arranging village level training programmes on crop production technology of soybean crop, which is now widely accepted short duration high yielding oilseeds crop followed by onion, garlic and tomato cultivation technology by organic farming methods. Marketing of produce attained the top most priority in assessing training needs (76 per cent), followed by plant protection (66 per cent) and manures and fertilizers (61 per cent). Vermicompost, its preparation and application methods accorded highest response (87 per cent) from the members followed by ITKs (81 per cent) being used in organic farming. Poultry farming ranked first (78 per cent) followed by agro-processing units (71 per cent) in the assessment of training needs. The respondents also desired to have training on priority in the field of agro-processing, dairy and kitchen yard gardening. The respondents felt the training needs on HRD and managerial aspects too. Communication skills ranked first (84 per cent) followed by access to infrastructural facilities like transport, water supply, school, marketing etc (81 per cent). Almost more than two third respondents indicated the training needs on the subjects like, conflict management, self confidence and self worth, participation in local affairs and meetings and community health and sanitation. The relational analysis showed that the selected variables like age, size of family, caste, income, land holding and social participation had positive and significant relationship with the training needs of the respondents while two variables namely education and type of family had negative relationship with training needs. The multiple regression analysis showed that out of eight independent variables, only age, and land holding contributed significantly towards the variation in the training needs of the respondents. The extent of variation was 52.88 per cent as the Co-efficient of Determination being 0.5288. The unexplained variation to the extent of 47.12 per cent may be attributed to the variables not included in the study.

17.2 Introduction

Following the success of Grameen Bank experiment in Bangla Desh, the strategy of forming Self Help Groups (SHGs) and extending micro-credit through them has been successfully adopted in India. SHG Bank Linkage Programme launched by NABARD in 1991-92, as an experiment in providing hassle free institutional credit to rural poor has achieved phenomenal success over last 15 years and is now acclaimed as largest micro credit programme in the world. The programme received further boost during 2003-04 in the country and Maharashtra is no exception to this. Maharashtra is the first state of the country to expand the Central Sector Scheme on "Women in Agriculture", which started on a pilot basis in Thane District to "One Taluka in each District". This scheme is being implemented by Mahila Arthic Vikas Mandal (MAVIM) and NGOs. The Department of Agriculture of Maharashtra State has been implementing the centrally sponsored scheme of Women in Agriculture through this innovative approach of SHGs, with the help of NGO in Sinnar Taluka of Nashik District since 2003-04. The main objective of the scheme is to enhance women's participation in agriculture in a very effective manner through technology transfer. Hence, village level training to the members of the women SHGs has been the major component of the scheme. Therefore, to impart the training in a very effective manner the identification of training needs of the tribal women SHG members has been of prime importance. Thus the present study was focused to identify training needs of the members of tribal women SHGs in the field of agriculture and to examine the relationship between training needs and personal, psychological and socio-economic characteristics of the members of women SHGs.

17.3 Materials and Methods

Since this study was confined to the operational area of the centrally sponsored scheme *viz* "Women in Agriculture", the Sinnar Taluka of Nashik District has been purposively selected for the same. A survey design involving observations at single time has been used for conducting this investigation. Thus Ex-post-facto research design was used for the study, since the researcher has no control over the independent variables. In view of the objectives of the study the Researcher has relied mainly on primary data collected from the randomly selected 100 members of the 50 Tribal Women SHGs through specially prepared interview schedule. The respondents were contacted personally. Data collected were tabulated and analyzed by using various statistical tools. The statistical methods used were correlation coefficient and multiple regression coefficients.

17.4 Results and Discussion

Assessment of Training Needs

For sustainable development of the group and individuals, the members should receive the training in almost all the fields like SHG orientation, agricultural activities, allied activities to agriculture, cottage industries, small business and services, access to infrastructural facilities, Human Resource Management and social development. In view of this and in order to priorities the training needs in these fields the responses of the members were collected in a specially designed interview schedules. The data has been compiled and analyzed and presented as follows:

Training Needs in SHG Orientation

It can be revealed from the Table 1, that almost more three fourth members prioritized their training needs in all the aspects of SHG orientation. Record keeping was most important training need since 81 per cent of the members opined it very much needed followed by training on SHG-Bank linkage programme (79 per cent). The members also desired to have training on conduct of group meetings, internal lending and role and responsibilities of the group leaders for successful running of SHGs.

Table 1: Assessment of Training Needs in SHG Orientation

n =100

Training Needs	*Very Much Needed (3)*		*Some What Needed (2)*		*Least Needed (1)*	
	No.	*Per cent*	*No.*	*Per cent*	*No.*	*Per cent*
Concept of SHG	76	76.00	21	21.00	03	03.00
Role and responsibilities of Members, Group Leaders	77	77.00	17	17.00	06	06.00
Conduct Group Meetings	78	78.00	18	18.00	04	04.00
Banking Operations	73	73.00	24	24.00	03	03.00
Internal Lending Rules and Roles	77	77.00	21	21.00	02	02.00
SHG-Bank Linkage	79	79.00	18	18.00	03	03.00
Record Keeping	81	81.00	16	16.00	03	03.00

Training Needs in Crop Production

It can be seen from the Table 2 that, the production techniques of food grains crops by and large stabilized in the area and hence the respondents have not indicated any urgent training need on these crops. However, more than three fourth (79 per cent) respondent have shown interest in knowing the production technology of soybean crop, which is now widely accepted short duration high yielding oilseeds crop. Similarly the Sinnar Taluka being pioneer in Onion and Garlic production the members have indicated the training needs for these crops by 83 and 63 per cent respectively. Tomato also seems to be very important cash crop, since 76 per cent of respondents wanted to know the latest production techniques of the same.

Table 2: Training Needs on Crop Production Technology

n =100

Training Needs	*Very Much Needed (3)*		*Some What Needed (2)*		*Least Needed (1)*	
Crop Production Technology	*No.*	*Per cent*	*No.*	*Per cent*	*No.*	*Per cent*
Bajra	51	51.00	21	21.00	28	28.00
Jowar	33	33.00	13	13.00	54	54.00
Paddy	19	19.00	18	18.00	63	63.00
Groundnut	39	39.00	36	36.00	25	25.00
Soybean	79	89.00	11	11.00	10	10.00
Wheat	53	53.00	38	38.00	09	09.00
Gram	36	36.00	17	17.00	47	47.00
Onion	83	83.00	17	17.00	00	00.00
Garlic	63	63.00	33	33.00	04	04.00
Tomato	76	76.00	24	24.00	00	00.00

Extent of Training Needs in the Subject Matter Areas

The Table 3 shows that that marketing of produce attained the top most priority in assessing training needs (76 per cent), followed by plant protection (66 per cent) and Manures and fertilizers (61 per cent).

Table 3: Extent of Training Needs in the important Subject Matter Areas of Crop Production

n =100

Training Needs	*Very Much Needed (3)*		*Some What Needed (2)*		*Least Needed (1)*	
Crop Production Technology	*No.*	*Per cent*	*No.*	*Per cent*	*No.*	*Per cent*
Land Preparation	31	31.00	44	44.00	25	25.00
Improved Varieties	56	56.00	41	41.00	03	03.00
Seeds and sowing	37	37.00	41	41.00	22	22.00
Manures and Fertilizers	61	61.00	32	32.00	07	07.00
Plant Protection	66	66.00	28	28.00	06	06.00
Irrigation	36	36.00	34	34.00	40	40.00
Weed Management	40	40.00	44	44.00	16	16.00
Use of Farm Implements and Machinery	60	60.00	33.	33.00	07	07.00
Harvesting of produce	56	56.00	43	43.00	01	01.00
Marketing	76	76.00	21	21.00	03	03.00

Assessment of Training Needs on Organic Farming and its Certification

It can be observed from the Table 4 that, the Vermi-compost, its preparation and application methods accorded highest response (87 per cent) from the members followed by ITKs (Indigenous Technical Knowledge, 81 per cent) being used in organic farming. This might only to reduce the ever increasing cost of production of different crops. By and large Training Needs in Organic farming methods and Its Certification was seen the top most priority amongst the members.

Table 4: Assessment of Training Needs on Organic Farming and its Certification

n =100

Training Needs	*Very Much Needed (3)*		*Some What Needed (2)*		*Least Needed (1)*	
Crop Production Technology	*No.*	*Per cent*	*No.*	*Per cent*	*No.*	*Per cent*
Concepts of Organic Farming	67	67.00	21	21.00	12	12.00
Organic farming systems	76	76.00	23	23.00	01	01.00
Indian local knowledge used in organic farming	81	81.00	19	19.00	00	00.00
Vermicompost	87	87.00	13	13.00	00	00.00
Biological control of pests	74	74.00	21	21.00	05	05.00
Certification process of organic farming system	76	76.00	13	13.00	11	11.00
Marketing of organic products	78	78.00	18	18.00	04	04.00

Assessment of Training Needs in Allied Activities to Agriculture and Agro Based Enterprises

Table 5: Assessment of Training Needs in Allied Activities to Agriculture and Agro-based Enterprises

n =100

Training Needs	*Very Much Needed (3)*		*Some What Needed (2)*		*Least Needed (1)*	
Crop Production Technology	*No.*	*Per cent*	*No.*	*Per cent*	*No.*	*Per cent*
Animal Husbandry and Dairy	62	62.00	29	29.00	09	09.00
Poultry Farming	78	78.00	19	19.00	03	03.00
Sheep and Goat Rearing	56	56.00	32	32.00	12.	12.00
Agro-processing Units	71	71.00	26	26.00	03	03.00
Agro-based small business and Services	55	55.00	36	36.00	09	09.00
Kitchen Yard Gardening	61	61.00	33	33.00	06	06.00

It can be revealed from the Table 5 that the Poultry farming ranked first (78 per cent) followed by Agro-processing units (71 per cent) in the assessment of training needs. In Sinnar taluka establishment of broiler poultry farms with the help of leading poultry industrial units like C and M. and Venkateshwara Hatcheries got very good momentum. Therefore, majority of the respondents have given priority in training needs in poultry. Similarly the training on agro-processing like cashew processing, masala making, papad and chatani making also accorded priority in the assessment in training needs. The respondents also desired to have training on priority in the field of Dairy and Kitchen yard gardening.

Assessment of Training Needs in Human Resource Development and Conflict Management in Social Participation

It could be observed from the Table 6 that the respondents felt the Training Needs on HRD and Managerial aspects too. Communication skills ranked first (84 per cent) followed by access to infrastructural facilities like transport, water supply, school, marketing etc (81 per cent). Almost more than two third respondents indicated the Training Needs on the subjects like, Conflict Management, Self confidence and Self Worth, Participation in Local Affairs and Meetings and Community Health and Sanitation.

Table 6: Assessment of Training Needs in Human Resource Development and Managerial Aspects

n =100

Training Needs	*Very Much Needed (3)*		*Some What Needed (2)*		*Least Needed (1)*	
Crop Production Technology	*No.*	*Per cent*	*No.*	*Per cent*	*No.*	*Per cent*
Communication Skills	84	84.00	16	16.00	00	00.00
Participation in local affairs and meetings	67	67.00	24	24.00	09	09.00
Resolving conflicts	79	79.00	19	19.00	02	02.00
Access to Infrastructural facilities	81	81.00	17	17.00	02	02.00
Community health and sanitation	78	78.00	18	18.00	04	04.00
Recognizing self worth	68	68.00	21	21.00	11	11.00

Relationship of Selected Independent Variables with Training Needs

To ascertain the relationship between Training Needs of the respondents and their selected socio-economic characteristics, the correlation co-efficient test was applied. The correlation co-efficient between Training Needs and various independent variables are presented in the following Table 7.

The results in Table 1 indicated that dependent variable "Training Need" exhibited non significant correlation with the independent variables namely education, type of family, social participation and annual income. However the dependent variable training need had significant correlation with age, size of family and caste, at 0.01 level of probability

Table 7: Relationship between respondent's Training Needs and Selected Independent Variables

Independent Variables	*Correlation Co-efficient (r)*
Age	0.607 **
Education	–0.458 NS
Size of Family	0.410 **
Type of Family	0.088 NS
Land Holding	0.322 **
Caste	0.210 **
Social Participation	–0.083 NS
Annual Income	0.164 NS

**: Significance at 0.01 level of probability; NS: Non Significant.

Multiple Linear Regressions of Training Needs with the Selected Independent Variables

Table 8: The Multiple Linear Regression of Training Needs with the Selected Independent Variables

Sl.No.	*Independent Variables*	*Regression Co-efficient (b)*	*'t' value of 'b'*
1.	Age	0.2196	5.09 **
2.	Education	– 0.2802	- 1.37 NS
3.	Size of Family	0.1063	0.45 NS
4.	Type of Family	0.1000	0.21 NS
5.	Land Holding	0.5066	2.19 *
6.	Caste	0.5959	1.87 NS
7.	Social Participation	– 0.1253	- 0.56 NS
8.	Annual Income	0.0000	0.76 NS

R^2 = 0.5288 Multiple Correlation = 0.6866; *: Significance at 0.05 level of probability.

**: Significance at 0.01 level of probability; NS: Non-significant.

It could be seen from above Table 8 that out of eight independent variables, only age, and land holding contributed significantly towards the variation in the Training Needs of the respondents. The extent of variation was 47.12 per cent as the co-efficient of Determination being 0.4712. The unexplained variation to the extent of 52.88 per cent may be attributed to the variables not included in the study. Thus, the Training Needs of the respondents about the various aspects of SHG functioning, farm and non-farm activities, Human Resource Development etc, were determined by the selected socio-economic characteristics. Among them, age and land holding were more prominent to decide requirement of the training needs of the respondents.

17.5 Conclusion

It can be concluded from the study that almost more three fourth members prioritized their training needs in all the aspects of SHG orientation. Record keeping was most important training need since 81 per cent of the members opined it very much needed followed by training on SHG-Bank linkage programme (79 per cent). It can be seen from the Table 2 that, the production techniques of food grains crops by and large stabilized in the area and hence the respondents have not indicated any urgent training need on these crops. However, more than three fourth (79 per cent) respondent have shown interest in knowing the production technology of soybean crop, which is now widely accepted short duration high yielding oilseeds crop. Similarly the Sinnar Taluka being pioneer in Onion and Garlic production the members have indicated the training needs for these crops by 83 and 63 per cent respectively. Tomato also seems to be very important cash crop, since 76 per cent of respondents wanted to know the latest production techniques of the same.

The members also desired to have training on conduct of group meetings, internal lending and role and responsibilities of the group leaders for successful running of SHGs (Table 3). It can be observed from the Table 4 that, the Vermi-compost, its preparation and application methods accorded highest response (87 per cent) from the members followed by ITKs (Indigenous Technical Knowledge, 81 per cent) being used in organic farming. This might only to reduce the ever increasing cost of production of different crops. By and large Training Needs in Organic farming methods and Its Certification was seen the top most priority amongst the members. It can be revealed from the Table 5 that the Poultry farming ranked first (78 per cent) followed by Agro-processing units (71 per cent) in the assessment of training needs. In Sinnar taluka establishment of broiler poultry farms with the help of leading poultry industrial units like C and M. and Venkateshwara Hatcheries got very good momentum. Therefore, majority of the respondents have given priority in training needs in poultry. Similarly the training on agro-processing like cashew processing, masala making, papad and chatani making also accorded priority in the assessment in training needs. The respondents also desired to have training on priority in the field of Dairy and Kitchen yard gardening. The results in Table 7 indicated that dependent variable "Training Need" exhibited non significant correlation with the independent variables namely education, type of family, social participation and annual income. However the dependent variable training need had significant correlation with age, size of family and caste, at 0.01 level of probability. It could be seen from above Table 8 that out of eight independent variables, only age, and land holding contributed significantly towards the variation in the Training Needs of the respondents. The extent of variation was 47.12 per cent as the co-efficient of Determination being 0.4712. The unexplained variation to the extent of 52.88 per cent may be attributed to the variables not included in the study. Thus, the Training Needs of the respondents about the various aspects of SHG functioning, farm and non-farm activities, Human Resource Development etc, were determined by the selected socio-economic characteristics. Among them, age and land holding were more prominent to decide requirement of the training needs of the respondents. In short, tribal farmwomen engaged with SHGs are needed trainings in each and every aspect of agriculture and Animal husbandry along with organic farming as a whole.

17.6 Suggestions/Implications

On the basis of findings and general observations emerged from the analysis of data, the following suggestions can be made in formulation of Training Curriculum for members of women Self Help Groups in agriculture.

1. **SHG Orientation** : SHG concept, Need of mutual help and working together with people's participation, Role and responsibilities of members and group leaders,Conduct of Group Meetings,Banking Operations and Nature of Transactions,Internal Lending : Rules and Roles,SHG-Bank Credit linkage, procedures and principles and Record Keeping.
2. **Crop Production**: Soybean cultivation practices,Onion production techniques, Garlic production and Tomato production and marketing.
3. **Subject Matter Areas**: Organic Farming methods,Vermi-compost, it's preparation and application,Bio-logical control of pests and diseases for Crop Protection,ITKs in Organic Farming,Certification procedures and Marketing of an organic produce.
4. **Non-farm Activities**: Poultry keeping,Animal Husbandry and Dairy,Sheep and Goat Keeping,Agro-processing,Agro-based Enterprises and Services and Kitchen Yard Gardening.
5. **Human Resource Development and Managerial Skills**: Communication Skills, Leadership Skills, Participation in Local Affairs and Meetings, Recognizing Self Worth, Resolving Conflicts, Access to the Infrastructural Facilities and Community Health and Sanitation.

References

Chaudhari, N. (2005), Breaking the Barriers (Sustainability of SHGs), Need for an Effective Facilitation, Theory and Practice of Micro-Finance, Department of Commerce and Management, Shivaji University, Kolhapur.

Chauhan,N.M. and Kshirsagar, S.M. (2012). Assessment of Training Needs of Members of tribal Women SHGs for Agriculture Development. *Ind. Res. J. of Ext. Edu. Special Issue (II), 2012. Page No. 193-198.*

Farooqui, H.F. (1992), Training Needs of Farmwomen. Maharashtra Journal of Agricultural Extension, 11, PP 257-262.

Harper, M. (2002), Promotion of Self Help Groups under the SHG-Bank Linkage Programme. Oxford / IBH New Delhi, ITDG Publications London.

Mangala Rai, (2004), Women in Agriculture, Annual Report of ICAR, Department of Agricultural Research and Education, PP 175-178.

NABARD, Maharashtra Regional Office, Pune (2005), Status Paper of Regional Workshop on Micro Finance at Shivaji University Kolhapur on 29th and 30th Jan, 2005

Puhazhendhi V, Badatya K.C. (2002), Self Help Groups Bank Linkage Programme for Rural Poor in India, An Impact Assessment. NABARD, Mumbai.

Puhazhendhi V, Satyasai K.J.S. (2000), Microfinance for rural people, NABARD, Mumbai.

Puhazhendhi V. (2000), Evaluation Study of Self Help Groups in Tamil Nadu NABARD, Mumbai.

Puhazhendhi, V and K.J.S.Satyasai (2000), Micro Finance for Rural people- An Impact Study, National Bank for Agriculture and Rural Development, Mumbai.

Chapter 18
Information Hungers of the Rice Growers

18.1 Abstract

The present investigation was confined to Anand district of Gujarat state. The information need of the 100 rice growers was measure using three point continuums. Major area of information needs as expressed by the rice growers in descending order of rank were Plant protection measures, Marketing, Schedule of water supply by Canal, Fertilizer management, Water management, Preparation of Seedlings, Variety, Land preparation and sowing, Supportive facts, Harvesting and post harvesting technology and Weed management. It was observed from the same table that majority of the rice growers have expressed their information needs about identification, nature of damage and control measures for insects/pests as well as diseases of rice crop; price of insecticides/pesticides; integrated pest management and method of preparing solutions of insecticides/pesticides. They articulated high need for information on market price followed by quality parameters that affects price and time of market inflow. It can be seen that the rice growers expressed their needs for information about subsidies, insurance and government policies related to rice cultivation.

18.2 Introduction

Rice is predominantly grown in Kheda district as it is the staple food crop of this region. The studies conducted in past in this region regarding rice crop production technology indicate that there is a wide gap exist between the knowhow already attained and their application in the fields. Thus, there is a wide scope for increasing production of rice per unit area. In order to increase the level of adoption, farmer must be made aware of the improved technologies.

Acquisition of information has always been regarded as a factor playing an important role in molding human behavior leading to decision for adopting of innovation. Mass dissemination of information may play an important role in increasing the adoption of technology. The preparation of good content of information of rice farming is possible based on the real information needs of the farmers. The content based on actual needs of the users will create interest among them to apply it in practice (Mehta, 2003). With a view to supporting larger group of rice growers with agricultural information in future, the present study was carried out with specific objective to ascertain the information needs of the rice growers. The golden era of an information age the high-tech rice production and marketing technologies should be reached to the final end users *i.e.* farmers. Hence, this attempt was made to study the information needs of the rice growers to increase rice production and income, too.

18.3 Methodology

The present investigation was confined to Anand district of Gujarat state. Anand district comprises of eight talukas. Khambhat is the major rice growing taluka of the district. This taluka was selected purposively because area under rice cultivation is highest among all the eight talukas of district. Five villages *viz;* Gudel, Galiyana, Naviakhol, Rohini, and Tamsa were selected randomly from among the list of the major rice growing villages of Khambhat taluka. The lists of rice growers were obtained for each of the selected villages from the gram panchayat office. Twenty respondents from each of the selected villages were randomly selected. Thus, the study was confined to 100 respondents. The information need of the farmer was measure using three point continuums. The mean score was obtained by the total number of score divided by total number of respondents.

18.4 Results and Discussion

(1) Information Hungers of the Rice Growers

The data presented in Table 1 revealed that major area of information needs expressed by the rice growers in descending order of rank were Plant protection measures, Marketing, Schedule of water supply by Canal, Fertilizer management, Water management, Preparation of Seedlings, Variety, Land preparation and sowing, Supportive facts, Harvesting and post harvesting technology and Weed management. The results are in conformity with the findings of Patel (2004). It means that the rice growers gave highest emphasis on market related information, as this information can help them to a great extent to convert their produce in more money. They were also conscious about information on schedule of water to be supplied by canal as well as plant protection measures. The data also reflects that the rice growers have become more cautious about fertilizer management due to new trend of organic rice framing. N. Prakash and Singh, (2010) also reported the same.

(2) Operation-wise Information Hungers of the Rice Growers

An attempt was made to ascertain operation wise information needs of the rice growers. The data in this regard are presented in Table 2 looking to the Variety, majority of the farmers have expressed their needs for information about sources of

Table 1: The Respondents According to their Overall Onformation Needs for Rice Cultivation

n = 100

Sl.No.	Areas of Information Needs	Mean Score	Rank
1.	Variety	1.31	V
2.	Schedule of water supply by Canal	1.67	II
3.	Preparation of Seedlings	1.36	IV
4.	Land preparation and sowing	1.22	VII
5.	Fertilizer management	1.67	II
6.	Weed management	0.71	XI
7.	Irrigation management	1.42	III
8.	Plant protection measures	1.89	I
9.	Harvesting and post harvesting technology	0.88	IX
10.	Marketing	1.89	I
11.	Supportive facts	1.21	VIII

Table 2: Information Needs of Paddy Growers

n = 100

Sl.No.	Areas of Information Needs	Mean Score	Rank
A.	**Variety of Paddy**		
1.	Source of seeds	1.63	I
2.	Suitable high yielding variety for the area	1.27	II
3.	Rate of seeds	1.12	III
4.	Characteristics of high yielding variety	0.67	IV
B.	Schedule of water to be supplied by Canal		
1.	Water to be supplied in channel before sowing time	1.82	I
2.	Time and date of supply of water in canal for complete crop period	1.27	II
C.	**Preparation of seedlings of Rice**		
1.	How to select site for raising seedlings	1.31	I
2.	Method of preparing bed for nursery	1.28	II
3.	Plant protection in nursery management	1.22	III
4.	Nutrient management in nursery	1.14	IV
5..	Proper age to select seedlings for transplanting	1.06	V
D.	**Sowing**		
1.	Seed rate	1.56	I
2	Sowing time	1.34	II
3	Depth of sowing	1.31	III

Contd...

Table 2–*Contd...*

Sl.No.	*Areas of Information Needs*	*Mean Score*	*Rank*
4.	Method of sowing	1.21	IV
5.	Spacing	1.11	V
6.	Seed treatment inputs	0.93	VI
E.	**Fertilizer management**		
1.	Price of fertilizers	1.82	I
2.	Method and time of fertilizer application	1.71	II
3.	Nutrient requirements of plant	1.41	III
4.	Calculating the doze of chemical fertilizer	1.40	IV
5.	Deficiency symptoms of major plant nutrients	1.32	V
6.	Bio-fertilizers	0.98	VI
F.	**Weed control**		
1.	Chemical weed control	0.93	I
2.	Price of weedicides	0.81	II
3.	Place of availability of weedicides	0.72	III
4.	Trade name of weedicides	0.61	IV
5.	Hand weeding	0.21	V
G.	**Irrigation management**		
1.	Schedule for irrigation	1.78	I
2.	Critical Stages of Irrigation	1.77	II
3.	How to save crop during shortage of water	1.66	III
4.	Fertilizer management during irrigation	1.21	IV
5.	Method of irrigation	0.41	V
H.	**Plant protection measures**		
1.	Identification, nature of damage and control measures for insects/pests of rice	1.73	I
2.	Identification, nature of damage and control measures for diseases of rice	1.71	II
3.	Price of insecticides and pesticides	1.53	III
4.	Integrated pest management in rice	1.22	IV
5..	Method of preparing solution of pesticides	1.05	V
I.	**Harvest and post harvest technology**		
1.	Proper time of harvest	1.21	I
2.	How to store rice production	1.09	II
3.	Care after harvesting at farm level	0.92	III
J.	**Marketing**		
1.	Market price	1.79	I
2.	Quality parameters that affects price	1.72	II

Contd...

Table 2–*Contd...*

Sl.No.	Areas of Information Needs	Mean Score	Rank
3.	Time of market inflow	1.67	III
4.	Place of marketing	1.52	IV
5.	Value addition	0.51	VII
K.	**Supportive facts**		
1.	Subsidies for rice cultivation	1.33	I
2.	Insurance of rice crop	1.16	II
3.	Government policies related to rice crop	1.04	III
4.	Credit/loan facilities for rice cultivation	0.89	IV

seeds, suitable high yielding variety for the area and rate of seeds. The reason might be that the farmers are convinced to sow good variety but the availability of seed of suitable variety and its' rate are always a dilemma for him. Schedule of water to be supplied by Canal, in the area of the study farmers are facing big dilemma of uncertain availability of the irrigation water through canal, thus they are facing problem of crop failure due to lack of expected irrigation water as and when required in required quantity. The Information about water to be supplied in canal before sowing time and advance information about time and date of supply of water in canal for complete crop period were the expected information needs of the rice growers.It is observed that due to lack of technical know-how farmers are not in position to prepare seedlings to transplant rice crop and faces problem in getting it as and when required. Some time due to unavailability of needed varieties' seedlings they grow unwanted variety of rice. Regarding Preparation of seedlings, the data presented in table gives us an idea that How to select site for raising seedlings, Method of preparing bed for nursery, Plant protection in nursery management, Nutrient management in nursery, Irrigation management in nursery and Proper age to select seedlings for transplanting were the major information realized by the rice growers. In case of land preparation and Sowing, the probable reason for high need for soil treatment related information might be due to the fact that the area encompasses high potentiality of irrigation mainly with canal. This resulted in accumulation of salts on the surface of soil, which forces the farmers to learn more about soil reclamation. Regarding fertilizer management the fertilizer management is indispensable for higher yields. The responses of the rice growers reveal that majority of them shown their interest of information on Price of fertilizers, Stock of fertilizers, Place of availability of fertilizers, Name of highly advantageous chemical fertilizers for rice, Method and time of fertilizer application, Nutrient requirements of plant, Calculating the doze of chemical fertilizer, Deficiency symptoms of major plant nutrients, Bio-fertilizers, Making organic manures. This means that the respondents know the importance of this input. It may help them in reducing the total cost of cultivation. Weed management is important non-monitoring inputs. Some of the least important needs expressed were Chemical weed control, Price of weedicides, Place of availability of feticides, Trade name of weedicides, Stock of weedicides and Hand weeding. The rice growers expressed that Schedule for irrigation, Critical Stages of Irrigation, How to save crop during shortage of water, Fertilizer management during irrigation and Method of irrigation were key areas of their need regarding irrigation management in rice crop. They realized that only by increasing the water use efficiency with the help of suitable method and time of irrigation, they can fetch good production of rice crop. That's why the rice growers had more in getting information related to irrigation. It was observed from the same table that majority of the rice growers have expressed their information needs about identification, nature of damage and control measures for insects/pests as well as diseases of rice crop; price of insecticides/pesticides; integrated pest management and method of preparing solutions of insecticides/pesticides. The probable reason for information needs about protection measures might be that this crop faces major problems in this regard and if plant protection is not done correctly, that may decrease production and increase the cost of cultivation. T. Manjunath, *et al.* (2011) reported the same.

Harvest and Post-harvest Technology

The data also shows that Proper time of harvest, Ideal thrasher for thrashings rice, How to store rice production; Care after harvesting at farm level and Care during harvesting were major information needs of rice growers.

Market

The rice growers expressed high information need for almost all the areas of market information. They articulated high need for information on market price followed by quality parameters that affects price and time of market inflow. The fluctuation in price of rice is very common mainly due to time of inflow, quality of rice and its' demand. Further, considerable variations between market yards are also observed. These leads rice growers to confirm high interest in the information regarding market so as to get maximum returns of their produces.

Supportive Facts

It can be seen that the rice growers expressed their needs for information about subsidies, insurance and government policies related to rice cultivation. The high cost of cultivation might have led the respondents to get information about subsidies. Similarly, high risk associated with the crop may force them to acquire information of insurance. The market price of rice depends greatly on government policies, which lead the farmers to know more about government policies including support price related to rice crop, declared from time to time.

18.5 Implication

It can be concluded that close collaboration with the extension worker should be thought of in order to impart training to the rice growers about improved technologies especially in the areas as expressed by them. Further, orientation of the training programme on how to make best use of the various sources of information may be organized which enables the rice growers to seek information. The high level, recent, updated and immediate availability of the information regarding rice growing and marketing as desired by farmers is need of the time for profitable rice cultivation in the country.

References

Chauhan, N.M. (2012). Information Hungers of the rice growers. *Agricultre Update*, vol.7 (1 and 2):72-75.

Mehta P.M, (2003).Information technology in agriculture paper presented at national workshop on ICT at DA-IICT, Gandhinagar.

N. Prakash and S.B. Singh, (2010).Adoption of zero tillage in Rice based cropping system in Manipur State, *Indian Res. J. Ext. Edu.*10(3):1-4.

Patel, D.D, (2004). Information needs of the Cotton growers. Unpublished M. Sc. Thesis submitted to Anand Agril. Uni. Anand.

SinghY.P,(2005). Adoption trends for improved rice technology Agril.Ext.Review.Vol.17:2005:17-18

T. Manjunath, L. Manjunath, K.V. natikar, K.A. jahagirdar and S.N. Megeri (2011). Paddy growers profile, knowledge and adoption of plant protection measures, Agric *Update*, Vol.6:21-27.

Chapter 19
Information on the Pay Attention of the Rice Growers

19.1 Abstract

The present investigation was confined to Anand district of Gujarat state. The information need of the 100 rice growers was measure using three point continuums. With a view to know the information behavior of the Rice growers, the study was undertaken in five villages of Anand district. Major area of information needs as expressed by the rice growers in descending order of rank were Plant protection measures, Marketing, Schedule of water supply by Canal, Fertilizer management, Water management, Preparation of Seedlings, Variety, Land preparation and sowing, Supportive facts, Harvesting and post harvesting technology and Weed management. The study concluded that use of information sources, extension participation, land under rice cultivation and cosmopoliteness were the important independent variables affecting information need of the rice growers. Majority of the respondents expressed plant protection measures, marketing, schedule of water supply by canal, fertilizer management and irrigation management as the important areas of information needs. N. Prakash and S.B. Singh, (2010) reported the results in this consistency.

It was observed from the same table that majority of the rice growers have expressed their information needs about identification, nature of damage and control measures for insects/pests as well as diseases of rice crop; price of insecticides/pesticides; integrated pest management and method of preparing solutions of insecticides/pesticides. They articulated high need for information on market price followed by quality parameters that affects price and time of market inflow. It can be seen that the rice growers expressed their needs for information about subsidies, insurance and government policies related to rice cultivation.

19.2 Introduction

Rice is the staple food of 65 per cent of the total population in India. It constitutes about 52 per cent of the total food grain production and 55 per cent of total cereal production. India became self sufficient in rice in 1977. That was achieved through a combination of increasing the area under cultivation and increasing cropping intensity. With the adoption of modern varieties in 1966, an average annual increase of 2 per cent in rice yield has been attained. Looking to the importance of the rice crop in the global economy the year 2004 was celebrated as International Rice Year T. Manjunath *et al.* (2011).

Increasing productivity is the vehicle for development of the rice sector. Rice production can be increased either by increasing the area under rice cultivation or by increasing the productivity of current cultivation. Given the pressure on agricultural land and the competition from other, more lucrative crops, it may be difficult to significantly increase the land under rice cultivation. The only solution, therefore, is to increase the productivity of the area currently under cultivation.

Mass dissemination of information may play an important role in view of its larger area coverage. Acquisition of information has always been regarded as a factor playing an important role in molding human behavior leading to decision for adopting of innovation. Thus, Identifying information needs of the users can become solid basis for developing meaningful information warehouse. Keeping in view the significance of the information needs of the rice growers the present study was undertaken with the following objectives.

1. To ascertain the information needs of the rice growers.
2. To study the relationship between selected personal, social, communicational, economical and psychological characteristics of rice growers and their information needs.

19.3 Methodology

The present investigation was confined to Anand district of Gujarat state. Anand district comprises of eight talukas. Khambhat is the major rice growing taluka of the district. This taluka was selected purposively because area under rice cultivation is highest among all the eight talukas of district. Five villages *viz;* Gudel, Galiyana, Naviakhol, Rohini, and Tamsa were selected randomly from among the list of the major rice growing villages of Khambhat taluka. The lists of rice growers were obtained for each of the selected villages from the gram panchayat office. Twenty respondents from each of the selected villages were randomly selected. Thus, the study was confined to 100 respondents. The information need of the farmer was measure using three point continuum.The mean score was obtained by the total number of score divided by total number of respondents. Coefficient of Correlation was computed to find out the relationship between each of the independent variables and the dependent variable.

19.4 Results and Discussion

(a) Information Need of the Rice Growers

The data presented in Table 1 revealed that major area of information needs expressed by the rice growers in descending order of rank were Plant protection measures, Marketing, Schedule of water supply by Canal, Fertilizer management, Water management, Preparation of Seedlings, Variety, Land preparation and sowing, Supportive facts, Harvesting and post harvesting technology and Weed management. The results are in conformity with the findings of Patel, (2004). It means that the rice growers gave highest emphasis on market related information, as this information can help them to a great extent to convert their produce in more money. They were also conscious about information on schedule of water to be supplied by canal as well as plant protection measures. The data also reflects that the rice growers have become more cautious about fertilizer management due to new trend of organic rice framing. Singh,(2005) also reported the same.

Table 1: Over all Information Needs of the Rice Growers

n= 100

Sl.No.	Areas of Information Needs	Mean Score	Rank
1.	Variety	1.31	V
2.	Schedule of water supply by Canal	1.67	II
3.	Preparation of Seedlings	1.36	IV
4.	Land preparation and sowing	1.22	VII
5.	Fertilizer management	1.67	II
6.	Weed management	0.71	IX
7.	Irrigation management	1.42	III
8.	Plant protection measures	1.89	I
9.	Harvesting and post harvesting technology	0.88	VIII
10.	Marketing	1.89	I
11.	Supportive facts	1.21	VII

(b) Correlation between Independent and Dependent Variables

The data presented in Table 2 clearly signify that information need of the rice growers had non-significant correlation with their age and education. This may be due to the fact that irrespective level of education, level of the rice growers had information need for rice cultivation remained indifferent. The information need of the rice growers had significant correlation with their extent of utilization of information sources. It indicates that those rice growers who utilize more information sources to acquire information regarding rice cultivation, have shown higher need for such information. This may be due to the fact that those who were using various sources of information might have understood importance of information regarding rice cultivation. Social participation of the rice growers had non-significant correlation with their information need. It reflects that social organizations of villages failed to motivate rice growers to decide difference between what is and what should be for higher production of rice.

Table 2: Correlation between Characteristics of Rice Growers and Information Need

n=100

Sl.No.	*Personal Traits*	*Correlation Coefficient Value*
1.	Age	0.011
2.	Education	0.141
3.	Use of information sources	0.192*
4.	Social participation	0.134
5.	Extension participation	0.281*
6.	Size of land holding	–0.021
7.	Land under rice cultivation	0.481*
8.	Irrigated area to total land	0.052
9.	Annual income	–0.112
10.	Cosmopoliteness	0.193*
11.	Economic motivation	-0.040
12.	Market orientation	0.114*

*: Significant at 0.05 per cent level of probability.

It is obvious from the result in the same table that the information need of the rice growers had significant correlation with their level of extension participation. It means that extension agencies played pivotal role in identifying rice growers' information needs. The probable reason for this might be that extension activities have been considered as an important source for getting information regarding agriculture certainly by those farmers, who were inquisitive to obtain information, took active part in extension activities.

Information need of the rice growers had non-significant correlation with their size of land holding. It shows that there were all most similar needs of the rice growers with small, medium and big size of land holdings. The probable reason might be that irrespective of the size of land holding, the rice growers always try to get maximum returns from their available resources. Further, the crop being profitable one, the farmers required to be updated with latest information that leads to stability in information need irrespective to the size of holding.

Information need of the rice growers had significant correlation with the proportionate land under rice cultivation of their total land. whereas it had non-significant correlation with their proportionate irrigated area to total land. The farmer, who covers big portion of his total land under rice cultivation, transmits more risk for this crop, which leads them to have more information to minimize risk factors. Any increase in irrigated area has no influence over information need of the rice grower. The findings are in line with the findings of Talati, (1994).

Information need of the rice growers had non-significant correlation with their annual income and level of economic motivation. It means that there was similar level of interest to have information on rice among rich and poor rice growers. The rice growers, with irrespective of annual income, will always have interest to increase their income that this factor might have led them to have information need for the rice cultivation technologies.

Information need of the rice growers had significant correlation with their level of cosmopoliteness as well as market orientation. The farmers with high level of cosmopolite ness tend to avail required information, which ultimately leads to less information need. It is also obvious that, all the rice growers want information of rice cultivation, irrespective of their orientation to market. Singh, (2005) also reported the same.

19.5 Conclusion

It can be concluded that majority of the rice growers had expressed plant protection measures; marketing, schedule of water supply by canal; fertilizer management and irrigation management are the important areas of information needs.

The independent variables like Use of information sources, Extension participation, Land under rice cultivation and Cosmopolite ness were significantly related with their information needs for rice cultivation. Rice growers who had better contact with sources of information, extension personals and more area under rice cultivation as well as high level of cosmopoliteness realized more information on various aspects of rice cultivation.

References

Chauhan, N.M. (2012). Information Impalement of Rice Growers.*Journal of Progressive Agriculture*, Vol-3, No.2, October-2012, PP: 29-32.

Mehta P.M, (2003).Information technology in agriculture paper presented at national workshop on ICT at DA-IICT, Gandhinagar.

N. Prakash and S.B. Singh, (2010).Adoption of zero tillage in Rice based cropping system in Manipur State, *Indian Res. J. Ext. Edu.*10(3):1-4.

Patel, D.D, (2004). Information needs of the Cotton growers. Un published M. Sc. Thesis submitted to Anand Agril. Uni. Anand.

SinghY.P,(2005). Adoption trends for improved rice technology Agril.Ext.Review.Vol.17:2005:17-18

Talati, J. P.1994. Training needs of banana growers of Kheda district of Gujarat state. Guj.J.Ext.Edu,(4 and 5):182

T. Manjunath, L. Manjunath, K.V. Natikar, K.A. Jahagirdar and S.N. Megeri,(2011). Paddy growers profile, knowledge and adoption of plant protection measures, Agric *Update*, Vol.6:21-27.

Chapter 20

Information Necessitates of the Rice Growers

20.1 Abstract

1. From this research it can be concluded that majority of the rice growers had middle age(52.00 per cent), up to secondary to higher secondary level of education (56.00 per cent),used fertilizer depot,neighbors an television as sources of information, low to medium level of social participation (74.00 per cent), medium level of extension contact(52.00 per cent), big size of land holding(53.00 per cent), 65 per cent of their total land holding under rice cultivation(64.00 per cent), 65 per cent of their total land under irrigation (66.00 per cent) and 50,000 to 10,000 rupees of annual income (52.00 per cent), while slightly more than two fifth of the rice growers had medium level of cosmopoliteness (42.00 per cent), economic motivation (41.00 per cent) and market orientation (45.00 per cent).
2. **Information needs of the rice growers:** Plant protection measures, Marketing, Schedule of water supply by Canal, Fertilizer management, Water management, Preparation of Seedlings, Variety, Land preparation and sowing, Supportive facts, Harvesting and post harvesting technology and Weed management.
   - ✰ Major information needs of rice growers about improved verities were sources of seeds, suitable high yielding variety for the area and rate of seeds.
   - ✰ The Information about water to be supplied in channel before sowing time and advance information about time and date of supply of water

in canal for complete crop period were the expected information needs of the rice growers relate for the canal irrigation mangers.

- ☆ How to select site for raising seedlings, Method of preparing bed for nursery, Plant protection in nursery management, Nutrient management in nursery, Irrigation management in nursery and Proper age to select seedlings for transplanting were the major information needs realized by the rice growers for nursery management in rice cultivation.
- ☆ The major areas information needs expressed by the rice growers about sowing of rice were land preparation, Soil treatment methods. Place of availability of soil treatment inputs, Seed rate, Price of soil treatment inputs, Sowing time, Depth of sowing, Method of sowing, Spacing, Seed treatment inputs and Gap filling.
- ☆ The major area of information needs related to fertilizer management were Price of fertilizers, Stock of fertilizers, Place of availability of fertilizers, Name of highly advantageous chemical fertilizers for rice, Method and time of fertilizer application, Nutrient requirements of plant, Calculating the doze of chemical fertilizer, Deficiency symptoms of major plant nutrients, Bio-fertilizers and procedure of making organic fertilizers.
- ☆ Some of the smallest amounts of information needs expressed by rice growers for weed management were Chemical weed control, Price of weedicides, Place of availability of weedicides, Trade name of weedicides, Stock of weedicides and Hand weeding.
- ☆ The rice growers expressed that Schedule for irrigation, Critical Stages of Irrigation, How to save crop during shortage of water, Fertilizer management during irrigation and Method of irrigation were key areas of their information needs regarding irrigation management in rice crop.
- ☆ The major rice information needs about plant protection measures expressed by rice growers were identification, nature of damage and control measures for insects/pests as well as diseases of rice crop; price of insecticides/pesticides; integrated pest management and method of preparing solutions of insecticides/pesticides.
- ☆ How to store rice production, Care after harvesting at farm level and Care during harvesting were major information needs of rice growers about harvesting and post harvest technology.
- ☆ Rice growers articulated high need for information on market price followed by quality parameters that affects price and time of market inflow.
- ☆ The rice growers expressed their needs for information on supportive facts like subsidies, insurance in rice crop and government policies related to rice cultivation.

3. The characteristics like Use of information sources, Extension participation, Land under rice cultivation and Cosmopoliteness were significantly related with their information needs for rice cultivation. In other words rice growers who had better contact with sources of information, extension personals and more area under rice cultivation as well as high level of cosmopoliteness realized more information on various aspects of rice cultivation.

20.2 Introduction

Agriculture is the strength of Indians economy, providing direct employment to about 70 per cent of working people in the country. It forms the basis of many premier industries of India, including the textile, jute, and sugar industries. Agriculture contributes about 31 per cent to GDP; about 25 per cent of India's exports are agricultural products.

Rice is the staple food of 65 per cent of the total population in India. It constitutes about 52 per cent of the total food grain production and 55 per cent of total cereal production. In our country both food and nonfood crops are grown. Food grains consist of cereals such as rice, wheat, jowar, bajra, and maize as well as pulses. Food crops grow on nearly 70 per cent of the gross sown area.

India became self sufficient in rice in 1977. That was achieved through a combination of increasing the area under cultivation and increasing cropping intensity. With the adoption of modern varieties in 1966, an average annual increase of 2 per cent in rice yield has been attained. About 55 percent of the rice area was planted to modern varieties in 1985. Rough rice production has exceeded 100 million tons annually since 1988; total production in 1994 was almost 120 million tones, with an average yield of 2.6 tons/ha. India regularly exports a small amount of high quality basmati (aromatic) rice. In 1995, India exported nearly 4.2 million tons of rice, in response to the large increase in demand in the world market.

Increasing productivity (*i.e.*, raising yields) is the vehicle for development of the rice sector. Rice production can be increased either by increasing the area under rice cultivation or by increasing the productivity of current cultivation. Given the pressure on agricultural land and the competition from other, more lucrative crops, it may be difficult to significantly increase the land under rice cultivation. In fact, this has actually decreased in the last seven years. The only solution, therefore, is to increase the productivity of the area currently under cultivation. This will lead not only to increased production but also to more efficient production. Three main factors affect rice productivity: irrigation; research and development and its extension to the farmer; and the availability of credit.

Research and development are crucial to create and deliver a package of technology suitable to the farmer's conditions. Particularly adaptive research is necessary to develop new technologies such as new high-yielding varieties, suited to particular conditions. For example, farmers in an area infested by a particular kind of pest should be able to use seed resistant to that pest. Similarly, farmers in drought-prone regions or in water-logged areas should use seed varieties that can withstand these conditions. The State should encourage the use of biotechnology to spur research of this kind. Furthermore, to be truly useful, the research carried out needs to be extended to the farmer. Effective extension services are extremely critical for improving rice yields. A large part of the credit for China's high rice yields goes to its well-developed extension system. Extension services include not only instructing farmers on the correct cropping 'package' they should use, but also educating them on good farm and crop management practices, *e.g.*, correct plant population density, appropriate post harvesting technologies, and correct water and soil management practices.

Information is considered as a critical input in decision-making if research and extension efforts. Information is known as power, those who own it. In contrast, lack of information causes uncertainty about the possible impact of decisions on results. Lack of accurate and timely information is one of the important factors for the inefficiency and imperfections observed in the agricultural marketing system in India. Now, 'Information' has started gaining importance. Besides the development of the theory of information, the need to have information systems to facilitate sound decisions in agriculture was greatly felt. There is a need to have an integrated system providing the required information to the various decision-makers at the right time and place.

Agriculture sector would demand for quickly approaching quite a larger area with a variety of information right from inputs, production and market intelligence. It is not feasible to reach in person regularly to every farmer to convey high tech farming techniques. Hence, the future extension strategy would concentrate on distant extension education by way of newspapers, radio, TV or electronic media. Further, all these media would require to carry information as per the demand of the producers.

The preparation of good content of information of rice farming is possible based on the real information needs of the farmers. The content based on actual needs of the users will create interest among then to apply it in practice. With a view to supporting larger group of rice growers with agricultural information in future, it seems worthwhile to determine the information needs of the rice growers.

20.3 Explanation of Problem

The research generates technologies that are carried by transfer of technology agents and thereby are used by farmers and ultimate users. It is claimed that quite a large number of technologies have been generated by the agricultural scientists which is very much useful to the farmers. Simultaneously, it is obvious that except few technologies including mainly some good crop cultivars, not many technologies have been either reached to the farms on a massive scale or the farmers really realized its contribution to increase production in short run or to increase sustainability in long run. The reasons may be many. Over and above the diverse situations prevailing in the fields as well as amongst the farmers, the capability of the farmers to purchase the inputs and non-availability of trustworthy inputs in time, high cost of purchased inputs and un-assured outcome from the farming and above all, the technologies that can be used by them are either not known to them at the time they need it or they lack proper understanding of the technologies so as to try it to their farm in a right manner.

It is needless to state that beyond producing appropriate technologies, it is equally important to take these technologies to all concerned.

This requires information management and its dissemination, training for knowledge and skill up gradation, providing platform for discussing, debating and making trial of the ideas and issues, etc. In addition to this, mass dissemination of information is also more important in view of its larger area coverage.

Acquisition of information has always been regarded as a factor playing an important role in molding human behaviour leading to decision for adopting of innovation. Identifying information needs of the users can become solid basis for developing meaningful information warehouse.

In Gujarat, number of new technologies for rice cultivation is generated. Till these technologies are taken to the farmers at the time they need it, the adoption rate would be low. Thus, for increased use of these technologies by the farmers, a right type of technology blended with right time would be required to be followed. Not only that the Khambhat taluka of Anand district carries significant area and production of rice in the district. There are more possibilities to harvest more. This is possible only if the farmers are provided with the information that is required by them, at the right time.

Keeping in view the significance of the information needs of the rice growers and as no study of this kind to assess the information needs of rice growers have been conducted in past, the present study was planned. The results of the study will form a basis for all those who are preparing contents for information to be transmitted to the rice growers for their use.

20.4 Objectives of the Study

The present study was undertaken with following objectives;

1. To study the profile of the rice growing farmers.
2. To ascertain the information needs of the rice growers.
3. To study the relationship between selected personal, social communicational, economical and psychological characteristics of rice growers and their information needs.
4. To suggest a model of technology transfer to cater the information needs of the rice growers.

20.5 Review of Literature

Reviews constitute an important source of information. It helps in clearing some concepts and improving focus help in avoidance of unnecessary duplication in research. In accordance with objectives of study the literature has been reviewed and presented as under

Patel (2004) reported that majority of the cotton growers expressed their needs for information about various aspects of marketing, water management, plant protection measures, fertilizer management and variety. Independent variables like use of information sources, extension participation, land under cotton cultivation and cosmopoliteness had significant correlation with information needs of the cotton growers.

Saini (1981) found that information need hierarchy were seed production, improved varieties, haymaking and fodder mixture and climatic requirements.

Stevens and Koch (1990) indicated that full and part time peach farmers in Silverton Extension ward did not differ significantly in their information needs.

Singh and Aggarwal (1993) found that information on harmful effects of drugs and smokeless chullah was most needed by Punjabi farmwomen. Fuel saving devices, time and energy saving devices and care and repair of household equipments were placed at third, fourth and fifth positions respectively.

Hanuman *et al.* (1997) reported that the tribal farmers had highest information needs about soil relation (78.00 MPS) where as the non-tribal farmers had the highest information needs about fertilizer application (74.17 MPS). It was also concluded that the tribal farmers had low information needs about use of biogas (30.34MPS) while the non-tribal farmers had poor information needs about fruits and vegetables (37.17MPS).

Sankar Rao and Reddy (1997) observed in their study on information needs of tribal farmers towards mango production technology that majority of the respondents (64.00 per cent) belonged to medium information need group followed by high (22.67 per cent) and low (13.33 per cent) information need group.

Pawar *et al.* (2001) observed that field crops and nursery management were considered as most important topics for information, followed by horticulture and farm development schemes.

Meera *et al.* (2003) found under *Gyandoot* Project (A ICT Project in M. P. State) that majority farmers perceived market information, facilitation of land record, question-answer services, information on Rural Development Programs and weather forecasting as the most important and essential information needs.

Singh *et al.* (1991) revealed that knowledge gap or citrus growers is negatively and significantly correlated with their extension contact.

Talati (1991) reported that education had significantly exerted their influence on training needs of banana growers of Kheda district. He also found that there was no significant influence of irrigation facilities on training needs to collect information on banana cultivation of banana growers of Kheda district with respect to improved banana cultivation technology.

Dolli and sudaraswmay (1994) revealed from their study on influence of socio-economic factors on technological information adoption gap in cultivation of pulse crop that there was negative and significant correlation between technological gap and extension contact.

Raut *et al.* (1995) observed in their study on influence of the characteristics of young farmers on their training needs to collection information about cultivation of fruit crops that education was significantly associated with training needs of the young farmers growing fruit crops.

Satpathy (1995) found that there was no significant association between age of the potato growers of kheda district and their training needs on the information of potato cultivation. He also observed negative and significant correlation between education of the potato growers and their training needs on the information of potato cultivation. At the same time revealed that there was negative and significant correlation of land holding and social participation with training needs on the information of potato cultivation. Of potato growers.

Vaghela (1996) revealed that age of the banana growers of anand taluka of kheda district had established positive and significant correlation (0.18699) with their training need to collect information on modern practices of banana. He further concluded that economic motivation of banana growers of anand taluka of kheda district had negative and significant correlation (-0.65954) with the training need to collect information on modern practices of banana.

Anonymous (2004) rice is the staple food for 65 per cent of the total population in india. The indian population was about 1 billion people in 2000 and is still growing at a high rate (1.7 per cent per year). Although the country exports several varieties of rice, many scientists have expressed concern that current indian rice production techniques cannot sustain the growing domestic population. India has a large number of rice dishes and many of them are very simple to prepare. Indian pilaf rice is very flavorful and fluffy when cooked with basmati rice.

Anonymous (2004) About 600 improved varieties of *indica* rice have been released for cultivation since 1965, but *Basmati* rice is still planted over large areas. Rice-based production systems provide the main income and employment for more than 50 million households.

Anonymous (2003) Rice is the main source of food for about half the world's population. Although it is cultivated world-wide, 91 percent is grown in Asia, which produces over 535 million metric tons of rice per year. On average, in the West, we consume 1.8 kg/4 lbs of rice per year per person, compared to 150 kg/330 lbs of rice per year per person in Asia.

20.6 Research Methodology

20.1.1 Location of Research Area

In view of limited resources available with the investigator, the present investigation was confined to Anand district of Gujarat state. The district is located in middle of the Gujarat From the total cultivable area large area is covered under irrigation. The principle crops of the district are tobacco, paddy, pearl millet, wheat and vegetable crops. Anand district comprises of eight talukas. Khambhat is the major rice growing taluka of the district. Thus study was undertaken in this taluka of the district. This taluka was selected purposely because area under rice cultivation is the highest among all the eight talukas of district.

20.1.2 Sample Size

In present investigation, simple random sampling technique was employed. First rice growing six villages *viz;* Gudel, Galiyana, Naviakhol, Rohini, Tamsa and Golana were selected to select respondents. The lists of rice growers were obtained for each of the selected villages from the gram panchayat office. It was planned to select almost 15 to 20 respondents from each of the selected villages randomly. Ultimately, a random sample of total of 100 respondents was selected for the study.

20.1.3 Research Design

As the study was concerned with understanding the information needs of rice growers, ex-post-facto research design was used for this study. This design was used because the researcher did not have any control on the independent variables of the selected rice growers.

Ex-post-facto research design is systematic experimental investigation in which control on independent variable is very weak and in this study all most no control was possible. Kerlinger (1976) stated that ex-pos-facto research design is worthy to apply when the independent variables have already acted up on.

20.1.4 Derivation of Hypothesis

On the basis of objective of the study, the following null hypothesis was formulated.

Ho- there will not be any relationship between selected characteristics of rice growers and their information needs.

20.1.5 Limitation of the study

On account of limited time and resources available with the investigator, the study was conducted with the following limitations:

1. The area of the study comprised to a few villages of Khambhat taluka of Anand district only. As such, the findings may be applicable only to the areas or places having similar agro-climatic conditions. A careful endeavor can help applying the findings of this study to other areas of the state.
2. The study was limited to 100 respondents.
3. The findings of the study were based upon the expression and responses of the rice growing farmers and its perception by the researcher. The validity of findings will therefore be limited to the extent the respondents are objective in their responses and the extent to which the researcher understood the responses correctly.

20.1.6 Method of Data Collection

An interview schedule was specially prepared and used as a tool for collection of requisite information. In all, 100 respondents were interviewed personally, with the help of the interviewed schedule. To avail correct and complete required information from respondents; an interview schedule was specifically structured keeping in view the objectives of the study. In formulating the questions and statements for schedule, the investigator sought the technical guidance from scientists/experts of the field and available literature and made it precise, clear and meaningful. The Data were collected by personal interview of the selected respondents. Every possible care was taken to seek an unbiased opinion of the respondents.

20.1.7 Selection of the Variable

The variables under study were selected on the basis of extensive review of literature related to the subject and consultation with experts and finally the variables that are found to be most relevant to the present study are selected as under.

20.1.7.1 Dependent Variables

1. Information needs of rice growers

20.1.7.2 Independent Variables

I. Personal Characteristics

(1) Age

(2) Education

II. Social-communicational Characteristics

(3) Use of information sources

(4) Social participation

(5) Extension participation

III. Economical Characteristics

(6) Size of land holding

(7) Land under rice cultivation

(8) Irrigated area to total land

(9) Annual income

IV. Psychological Characteristics

(10) Cosmopoliteness

(11) Economic motivation

(12) Market orientation

20.7 Measurement of Variables

20.7.1 Dependent Variable

20.7.1.1 Ascertaining Information Needs

The information needs of the rice growers were assessed for the areas right from the requirements for selection of crop and variety, through the availability of inputs, production technologies, harvesting and packaging; till farm level processing and marketing of the produce. Various related items were selected for these areas by reviewing the literature and a final shape was given after getting the opinion of the experts. Thus, the information needs of rice grower farmers about various aspects of rice cultivation were ascertained. The extent of information needs of the rice growers was availed on a three-point continuum ranging from most needed, needed and not needed. The three categories were assigned with 2 score, 1 score and 0 score respectively. The information needs were worked out for each of the major areas considering the total score for information need acquired by the respondents. On the basis of the mean score, the ranks to the major areas of information needs were assigned.

20.7.2 Measurement of Independent Variables

20.7.2.1 Age

Age refers to the total number of years completed by the respondents at the time of interview. The respondents were asked for their age in terms of completed years. The age in years as such was considered as the age score for each respondent. They were grouped in to three categories *viz;* Young (Up to 30 years), Middle (31 to 50 years) and Old aged (Above 50 years)

20.7.2.2 Education

It was operationalised as the level of formal schooling completed by the respondents. For each category, the scoring was assigned as per socio-economic scale of Pareek and Trivedi (1965), with due modifications. The one score for each year of the formal education was assigned to work out strength of this variable. They were classified in to five groups *viz;* Illiterate, Can read and write, Primary education (1st to 7th std.), Secondary/Higher Secondary education (8th to 12 std.) and College and above education.

20.7.2.3 Use of Information Sources

Communication sources were conceptualizes as the sources through which Gujarat farmers get information about improved agricultural technologies, especially in regard to rice cultivation. To measure the degree of utilization of the sources, each respondent was asked to indicate; as to how often he accessed information about rice cultivation from each of the sources. Score of 2, 1 and 0 was assigned for each of the respondent, for response in terms of often, some times and never respectively. The mean score was worked for each source to know degree of its use.

20.7.2.4 Social Participation

Social participation in the present study was operationalised as the degree to which an individual was associated with different social organizations either as a member or its office bearer. One score was given for having membership in each organization and 2 score for holding position in each organization; whereas, 0 score was given for non-membership in any organization. The total score obtained by each respondent was considered for studying the variable. On the basis of total score, the respondents were grouped into three categories *viz.* low (below mean – 0.5 S. D.), medium (in between mean $\pm$ 0.5 S. D.) and high (above mean + 0.5 S. D.)

20.7.2.5 Extension Participation

Extension participation is defined as the degree to which an individual participates in various non-formal extension activities, with a view to obtain new information, knowledge and skills related to agriculture. One score was given for participating in each of the extension activity. The respondents were grouped into three categories *viz.* low (below mean – 0.5 S. D.), medium (in between mean ± 0.5 S. D.) and high (above mean + 0.5 S. D.).

20.7.2.6 Size of Land Holding

Land holding is an important factor that determines the economic status and potentiality of an individual respondent. It refers to the number of hectares of land owned and cultivated by the respondents. Land possessed by an individual including irrigated and un-irrigated land was considered as total size of land holding. After getting the total land holding of individual respondents, they were classified in to four categories *viz;* Marginal farmers (Up to 1.00 hectare), Small farmers (1.01 to 2.00 hectares), Medium farmers (2.01 to 4.00 hectares) and Big farmers (Above 4.00 hectares)

20.7.2.7 Land Under Rice Cultivation

The area under rice cultivation in hectares possessed by the respondents was considered for measuring this variable. Expert opinion was obtained for deciding range for classification of the respondents. Considering the opinion received from 25 experts, the respondents were grouped in to three categories; land under rice crop Up to 35.00 per cent, 35.01 to 65.00 per cent and Above 65.00 per cent of total land.

20.7.2.8 Irrigated Area to Total Land Holding

The proportion of irrigated area to total land holding of the respondents in hectares was considered for measuring this variable. Expert opinion was obtained for deciding range for classification of the respondents. Considering the opinion received from 25 experts, the respondents were grouped *viz;* land under irrigation Up to 35.00 per cent, 35.01 to 65.00 per cent and Above 65.00 per cent of total land.

20.7.2.9 Annual Income

This refers to the total annual earnings of the respondents through all sources. It was measured in terms of range and grouped into three categories *viz;* Low (Up to Rs. 50,000/- Medium (Rs. 50,001 to Rs. 100,000/-) and High (Above Rs. 100,000/-)

20.7.2.10 Cosmopoliteness

Cosmopoliteness is the tendency of an individual to be in contact with outside his own community, based on the belief that individuals all the needs cannot be satisfied within his own community. This was measured with the help of scale developed by Singh (1973). The total score for individual respondents was obtained by adding all the scores of the statements as suggested in scale. The sum of score attained for classifying into three groups *viz;* Low level of cosmopoliteness (Below mean - 0.5 SD), Medium level of cosmopoliteness (Mean ± 0.5 SD) and High level of cosmopoliteness (Above mean + 0.5 SD).

20.7.2.11 Economic Motivation

This was measured with the help of economic motivation scale worked out by Supe (1969). Economic motivation score of an individual respondent was the sum of the scores of all the statements included in the scale. Categories formed on the basis of mean and standard deviation; *viz;* Low level (Below mean - 0.5 SD), Medium (Mean ± 0.5 SD) and High level of economic motivation (Above mean + 0.5 SD).

20.7.2.12 Market Orientation

The scale used to measure this variable is based on market orientation scale developed by Samantha (1977). Total score was obtained by summing all the responses. High score indicated high degree of market orientation in this scale. Conceptually, the respondents were categorized into three groups on the basis of mean and standard deviation; Low level of market orientation (Below mean - 0.5 SD), Medium level of market orientation (Mean $\pm$ 0.5 SD) and High level of market orientation (Above mean + 0.5 SD).

20.8 Statistical Framework for the Analysis of Data

The following statistical tools were used for interpreting the data.

20.8.1 Frequency and Percentage

Simple comparisons were made on the basis of frequency and percentage.

20.8.2 Mean

The mean was obtained by the total number of score divided by total number of trainees.

20.8.3 Coefficient of Correlation

Coefficient of Correlation was computed to find out the relationship between each of the independent variable and the dependent variable by employing following formula.

$$r = \frac{N\Sigma XY - \Sigma X \Sigma Y}{\sqrt{\left[(\Sigma N \Sigma X)^2 - (\Sigma X)^2\right]\left[(\Sigma N \Sigma Y)^2 - (\Sigma Y)^2\right]}}$$

where,

r: Correlation coefficient
X: Independent variable
Y: Dependent variable
N: Total number of respondents

20.9 Results and Discussion

The data pertaining to the present investigation were collected, classified, tabulated, analyzed and presented in succeeding pages under following heads:

20.9.1 Characteristics of the Rice Growers

Information assumes value in a decision-making context. Information needs may depend on personal traits of rice growers. Personal traits in this study, includes personal characteristics, social-communicational characteristics, economical characteristics and psychological characteristics of rice growers. An attempt has been made to analyze some of the personal characteristics like age and education; social communicational characteristics like use of information sources, social participation and extension participation; economical characteristics like size of land holding, land under rice cultivation, irrigated area to total land and annual income; psychological characteristics like cosmopoliteness, economic motivation and market orientation. The results obtained in this investigation are presented as under:

20.9.1.1 Age

Age is an important factor, which might have some influence on the behavior pattern of the rice growers. Generally, it is believed that young farmers are active and dynamic. The data presented in the Table 3 reflect that more than half of the respondents (52.00 per cent) were in the middle age group followed by old age group (36.00 per cent) and young age group (12.00 per cent).

Table 1: The Respondents According to the Age

n = 120

Sl.No.	*Age Group*	*Number*	*Per cent*
1.	Young	12	12
2.	Middle	52	52
3.	Old	36	36
	Total	**100**	**100**

From the Table 1, it can be concluded that majority of the rice growers were from middle to old age group. Since, we studied rice growers and probably the younger generation may be occupied elsewhere; the old age group generation is taking care of the farming.

20.9.1.2 Education

Education helps to broaden the vision of an individual, thereby facilitate in the process of producing desired changes in the behavior of the people. Information about formal education received by the respondents was collected and presented in Table 2.

Table 2: The Respondents According to the Level of Education

n = 120

Sl.No.	*Education Level*	*Number*	*Per cent*
1.	Illiterate	03	03
2.	Can read and write	05	05
3.	Primary education	22	22
4.	Secondary/Higher Secondary education	56	56
5.	College and above education	14	14
	Total	**100**	**100**

The data presented in Table 2 revealed that majority of the respondents (56.00 per cent) had education up to secondary to higher secondary level, followed by 22.00

per cent and 14.00 per cent with up to primary and college level respectively. Very few of them (4.03 per cent) have ability to read and write and only 3.00 per cent were illiterate. It can be concluded that majority of the rice growers had up to secondary level of education and above. This may be due to awareness about importance of education in life.

20.9.1.3 Use of Information Sources

With a view to studying the sources of information used by the rice growers for getting information related to rice cultivation, the data were collected, analyzed and presented in Table 3. It indicated that major formal sources of information preferred and utilized by the rice growers were fertilizer depot and Service co-operative societies. In case of informal sources like neighbors, friends or progressive farmers were utilized by them. In case of mass media, they exploited TV, News Papers, Radio, Agricultural Exhibition and printed literatures.

Table 3: The Respondents According to the Use of Information Sources

n = 100

Sl.No.	*Sources of Information*	*Mean Score*	*Rank*
A.	**A Formal Sources**		
1.	Fertilizer Depot.	1.81	I
2.	Service of co-operative society	1.78	II
3.	Village level worker	0.74	III
4.	SMS/Sub-divisional officer	0.56	IV
5.	Agricultural Research Scientists	0.21	V
B.	**Formal Sources**		
1.	Neighbors	1.88	I
2.	Friends/Relatives	1.76	II
3.	Progressive farmers	0.89	III
C.	**Mass Media**		
1.	TV	1.67	I
2.	News paper	1.41	II
3.	Radio	1.32	III
4.	Agricultural Exhibition/fair	1.31	IV
5.	Printed literature	0.61	V

20.9.1.4 Social Participation

An attempt was made to study the degree of association of the respondent with nearby social organizations. The data regarding social participation are presented in Table 4.

The data revealed that 44.00 per cent of the respondents had medium level of social participation followed by 30.00 per cent with low level and 26.oo per cent with high level of social participants.

Table 4: The Respondents According to their Level of Social Participation

n = 100

Sl.No.	*Social Participation*	*Number*	*Per cent*
1.	Low	30	30
2.	Medium	44	44
3.	High	26	26
	Total	**100**	**100**

20.9.1.5 Extension Participation

Participation in various extension activities helps an individual to learn more about the technology and also to acquire more information. An attempt was also made to study the level of extension participation of the respondents. The data regarding extension participation are presented in Table 5.

Table 5: The Respondents According to Level of Extension Participation

n = 100

Sl.No.	*Extension Participation*	*Number*	*Per cent*
1.	Low	24	24
2.	Medium	52	52
3.	High	24	24
	Total	**100**	**100**

The data in Table 5 reflected that 52.00 per cent of the respondents had medium level of extension participation and at the same time an equal per cent (24.00 per cent) of the respondents had low and high level of extension participation. It can be concluded that about fifty per cent of the respondents had medium level of extension participation. This reflects good interest of the respondents to participate in extension activities.

20.9.1.6 Size of Land Holding

Land holding has been considered as one of the important variables that determines the economic status and potentiality of farmers to go for modern technology. In view of this, farm size of the respondents was studied and data are presented in Table 6. Table reveals that majority (53.00 per cent) of the respondents had big size of land holding, followed by 22.00,14.00 and 11.00 per cent with medium, small and marginal size of land holding. From this, it can be concluded that majority of the respondents had above 4 hectares of land holding.

Not only total land holding, but the proportionate area under rice cultivation also affects the information needs of rice growers. Area under rice cultivation in proportion to the total land possessed by the respondents was considered for measuring this variable. The data regarding land under rice cultivation are presented in Table 7.

Table 6: The Respondents According to Size of Land Holding

n = 124

Sl.No.	Category	Number	Per cent
1.	Marginal Size (Up to 1 ha.)	11	11
2.	Small Size (1.01 to 2 ha.)	14	14
3.	Medium Size (2.02 to 4 ha.)	22	22
4.	Big Size (Above 4 ha.)	53	53
	Total	**100**	**100**

20.9.1.7 Land Under Rice Cultivation

Data presented in Table 7 revealed that 64.00 per cent of the respondents had above 65 per cent, 24.00 per cent had in between 35.01 to 65.00 per cent and 12.00 per cent of them had up to 35 per cent of their total land holding under rice cultivation.

Table 7: The Respondents According to the Land Under Rice Cultivation

n = 100

Sl.No.	Land Under Rice Cultivation	Number	Per cent
1.	Up to 35.00 per cent	12	12
2.	35.01 to 65.00 per cent	24	24
3.	Above 65 per cent	64	64
	Total	**100**	**100**

20.9.1.8 Irrigated Area to Total Land

It is visualized that a farmer having more area under irrigation may go for more commercialized approach to farming. This may need for more information. The information with regard to irrigated area to total land holding was considered in terms of proportion. The data collected in this regard are presented in Table 8.

Table 8: The Respondents According to the Proportion of Irrigated Land

n = 100

Sl.No.	Proportion of Irrigated Land	Number	Per cent
1.	Up to 35.00 per cent	08	08
2.	35.01 to 65.00 per cent	26	26
3.	Above 65 per cent	66	66
	Total	**100**	**100**

Data depicted in Table 8 reflect that that 66.00 per cent of the respondents had above 65 per cent, 26.00 per cent had in between 35.01 to 65.00 per cent and 08.00 per cent of them had up to 35 per cent of their total land holding under irrigation.

20.9.1.9 Annual Income

Annual income refers to the quantum of money earned by farmers during the year from farm and non-farm sources. Data regarding annual income of respondents were collected and presented in Table 9. It can be seen that majority (52.00 per cent) of the rice growers had medium (Rs. 50,001 to Rs. 100,000/-), followed by 34.00 per cent with high (Above Rs. 100,000/-) and 14.00 per cent with low (Up to Rs. 50,000/-) level of annual income. The medium to big size of land holding with majority of respondents under irrigated farming might be the reason for above findings.

Table 9: The Respondents According to the Level of Income

n = 100

Sl.No.	Level of Income	Number	Per cent
1.	Low (Up to Rs. 50,000/-)	14	14
2.	Medium (Rs. 50,001 to Rs. 100,000/-)	52	52
3.	High (Above Rs. 100,000/-)	334	34
	Total	**100**	**100**

20.9.1.10 Cosmopoliteness

This psychological character of the respondents was studied to know their tendency to be in contact with sources, outside of their community/area for getting more information. The collected data are presented in Table 10. The data in Table clearly indicate that slightly more than two fifth of the respondents (42.00 per cent) had medium level of cosmopoliteness. This was followed by 37.00 per cent and 21.00 per cent respondents with low and high level of cosmopoliteness, respectively.

Table 10: The Respondents According to the Level of Cosmopoliteness

n = 100

Sl.No.	Level of Cosmopoliteness	Number	Per cent
1.	Low	37	37
2.	Medium	42	42
3.	High	21	21
	Total	**100**	**100**

20.9.1.11 Economic Motivation

It refers to the occupational excellence in terms of profit making and relative value placed on economic ends by the farmers. The data in this regard were collected and are presented in Table11. The data revealed that 41.00 per cent of the respondents had medium level of economic motivation followed by 34.00 per cent had low level of economic motivation. There were 25.00 per cent of the respondents, who had high level of economic motivation.

Table 11: The Respondents According to the Level of Economic Motivation

n = 100

Sl.No.	*Level of Economic Motivation*	*Number*	*Per cent*
1.	Low	34	34
2.	Medium	41	41
3.	High	25	25
	Total	**100**	**100**

20.9.1.12 Market Orientation

The market orientation is such a psychological trait that is associated with his need for market related information. This helps the farmer to analyze the market intelligence to avail better price. The data regarding level of market orientation of the respondents are presented in Table 12. The Table revealed that 45.00 per cent of the respondents had medium level of market orientation. This was followed by 31.00 per cent and 24.00 per cent of the respondents with low and high level of market orientation, respectively.

Table 12: The Respondents According to the Level of Market Orientation

n = 100

Sl.No.	*Level of Market Orientation*	*Number*	*Per cent*
1.	Low	31	31
2.	Medium	45	45
3.	High	24	24
	Total	**100**	**100**

20.9.2 Information Needs of the Rice Growers

An attempt was made to ascertain information needs of the rice growers. This included information needs about variety, land preparation and sowing, fertilizer management, weed management and inter-culturing, water management, plant protection measures, harvesting and post harvest technology, marketing and supportive facts. The data in this regard are presented in Table 13.

The data in Table 13 revealed that major area of information needs expressed by the rice growers in descending order of rank were Plant protection measures, Marketing, Schedule of water supply by Canal, Fertilizer management, Water management, Preparation of Seedlings, Variety, Land preparation and sowing, Supportive facts, Harvesting and post harvesting technology and Weed management.

This means that the rice growers gave highest emphasis on market related information, as this information can help them to a great extent to convert their produce in more money. They were also conscious about information on schedule of water to be supplied by canal as well as plant protection measures. The data also reflects that the rice growers have become more cautious about fertilizer management due to new trend of organic rice framing.

Table 13: The Respondents According to their Over all Information Needs for Rice Cultivation

n = 100

Sl.No.	Areas of Information	Mean Score	Rank
1.	Variety	1.31	V
2.	Schedule of water supply by Canal	1.67	II
3.	Preparation of Seedlings	1.36	IV
4.	Land preparation and sowing	1.22	VII
5.	Fertilizer management	1.67	II
6.	Weed management	0.71	IX
7.	Irrigation management	1.42	III
8.	Plant protection measures	1.89	I
9.	Harvesting and post harvesting technology	0.88	VIII
10.	Marketing	1.89	I
11.	Supportive facts	1.21	VII

20.9.2.1 Information Needs about Variety

The information needs of rice growers about various aspects of variety were ascertained and recorded in Table 14.

The data presented in Table 14 indicate that majority of the farmers have expressed their needs for information about sources of seeds, suitable high yielding variety for the area and rate of seeds. The reason might be that the farmers is convinced to sow good variety but the availability of seed of suitable variety and its' rate are always a dilemma for him.

Table 14: The Respondents According to Information Needs about Variety

n = 100

Sl.No.	Areas of Information	Mean Score	Rank
1.	Source of seeds	1.63	I
2.	Suitable high yielding variety for the area	1.27	II
3.	Rate of seeds	1.12	III
4.	Stock of seeds	0.89	IV
5.	Characteristics of high yielding variety	0.67	V

20.9.2.2 Information Needs about Schedule of Water to be Supplied by Canal

In the area of the study farmers are facing big dilemma of uncertain availability of the irrigation water through canal, thus they are facing problem of crop failure due to lack of expected irrigation water as and when required in required quantity. The

Information about water to be supplied in canal before sowing time and advance information about time and date of supply of water in canal for complete crop period were the expected information needs of the rice growers as seen in Table 15.

Table 15: Information Needs about Schedule of Water to be Supplied by Canal

n = 100

Sl.No.	*Areas of Information*	*Mean Score*	*Rank*
1.	Information about water to be supplied in channel before sowing time	1.82	I
2.	Advance information about time and date of supply of water in canal for complete crop period	1.27	II

20.9.2.3 Information Needs about Preparation of Seedlings of Rice

It is observed that due to lake of technical know-how farmers are not in position to prepare seedlings to transplant rice crop and face problem in getting it as and when required. Some time due to unavailability of needed varieties' seedlings they grow unwanted variety of rice. Thus information need was studied in this regard and data are presented in Table 16. The Table gives us an idea that How to select site for raising seedlings, Method of preparing bed for nursery, Plant protection in nursery management, Nutrient management in nursery, Irrigation management in nursery and Proper age to select seedlings for transplanting were the major information realized by the rice growers.

Table 16: Information Needs about Preparation of Seedlings of Rice

n = 100

Sl.No.	*Areas of Information*	*Mean Score*	*Rank*
1.	How to select site for raising seedlings	1.31	I
2.	Method of preparing bed for nursery	1.28	II
3.	Plant protection in nursery management	1.22	III
5.	Nutrient management in nursery	1.14	IV
4.	Irrigation management in nursery	1.11	V
5.	Proper age to select seedlings for transplanting	1.06	VI

20.9.2.4 Information Needs about Land Preparation and Sowing

The information needs of the rice growers about various aspects of land preparation and sowing were documented and presented in Table 17. It is evident from the data that major areas information needs expressed by the rice growers were land preparation, Soil treatment methods. Place of availability of soil treatment inputs, Seed rate, Price of soil treatment inputs, Sowing time, Depth of sowing, Method of sowing, Spacing, Seed treatment inputs and Gap filling

Table 17: The Respondents According to Information Needs about Land Preparation and Sowing

n = 100

Sl.No.	*Areas of Information*	*Mean Score*	*Rank*
1.	Land preparation	1.67	I
2.	Soil treatment methods	1.61	II
3.	Place of availability of soil treatment inputs	1.56	III
4.	Seed rate	1.56	IV
5.	Price of soil treatment inputs	1.51	V
6.	Sowing time	1.34	VI
7.	Depth of sowing	1.31	VII
8.	Method of sowing	1.21	VII
9.	Spacing	1.11	IX
10.	Seed treatment inputs	0.93	X
11.	Gap filling	0.32	XI

The probable reason for high need for soil treatment related information might be due to the fact that the area encompasses high potentiality of irrigation mainly with canal. This resulted in accumulation of salts on the surface of soil, which forces the farmers to learn more about soil reclamation.

20.9.2.5 Information Needs about Fertilizer Management

The fertilizer management is indispensable for higher yields. Therefore information needs of the rice growers about various aspects of fertilizer management were studied and the results are presented in Table 18. The data reveal that majority

Table 18: The Respondents According to Information Needs about Fertilizer Management

n = 100

Sl.No.	*Areas of Information*	*Mean Score*	*Rank*
1.	Price of fertilizers	1.82	I
2.	Stock of fertilizers	1.78	II
3.	Place of availability of fertilizers	1.74	III
4.	Name of advantageous chemical fertilizers for rice	1.72	IV
5.	Method and time of fertilizer application	1.71	V
6.	Nutrient requirements of plant	1.41	VI
7.	Calculating the doze of chemical fertilizer	1.40	VII
8.	Deficiency symptoms of major plant nutrients	1.32	VIII
9.	Bio-fertilizers	0.98	IX
10.	Making organic matter from farm waste	0.87	X
11.	Organic manures	0.62	XI

of the rice growers shown their interest of information on Price of fertilizers, Stock of fertilizers, Place of availability of fertilizers, Name of highly advantageous chemical fertilizers for rice, Method and time of fertilizer application, Nutrient requirements of plant, Calculating the doze of chemical fertilizer, Deficiency symptoms of major plant nutrients, Bio-fertilizers, Making organic. This means that the respondents know the importance of this input. The information regarding foresaid aspects may help them reducing the total cost of cultivation.

20.9.2.6 Information Needs about Weed Management

Weed management is important non-monitoring inputs. The information needs of the rice growers about weed management were ascertained and presented in Table 19; the respondents did not express their higher needs for this particular practice of paddy cultivation. All though some of the least important needs expressed were Chemical weed control, Price of weedicides, Place of availability of weedicides, Trade name of weedicides, Stock of weedicides and Hand weeding.

Table 19: The Respondents According to Information Needs about Weed Management

n = 100

Sl.No.	Areas of Information	Mean Score	Rank
1.	Chemical weed control	0.93	I
2.	Price of weedicides	0.81	II
3.	Place of availability of weedicides	0.72	III
4.	Trade name of weedicides	0.61	IV
5.	Stock of weedicides	0.42	V
6.	Hand weeding	0.21	VII

20.9.2.7 Information Needs about Irrigation Management

Out of the total cultivable area of Khambhat taluka, 60 per cent is under canal irrigation. The rice is major crop in this Taluka of Anand district. Rice is one of the crops which require highest water to survive. As such, the information needs of the rice growers about irrigation management was identified and presented in Table 20.

Table 20: Respondents According to Information Needs about Irrigation Management

n = 100

Sl.No.	Areas of Information	Mean Score	Rank
1.	Schedule for irrigation	1.78	I
2.	Critical Stages of Irrigation	1.77	II
3.	How to save crop during shortage of water	1.66	III
4.	Fertilizer management during irrigation	1.21	IV
5.	Method of irrigation	0.41	V

The rice growers expressed that Schedule for irrigation, Critical Stages of Irrigation, How to save crop during shortage of water, Fertilizer management during irrigation and Method of irrigation were key areas of their need regarding irrigation management in rice crop. They realized that only by increasing the water use efficiency with the help of suitable method and time of irrigation, they can fetch good production of rice crop. That's why the rice growers had more in getting information related to irrigation.

Table 21: Respondents According to Information Needs about Plant Protection Measures

n = 100

Sl.No.	Areas of Information	Mean Score	Rank
1.	Identification, nature of damage and control measures for insects/pests of rice	1.734	I
2.	Identification, nature of damage and control measures for diseases of rice	1.710	II
3.	Price of insecticides and pesticides	1.532	III
4.	Integrated pest management in rice	1.226	IV
6.	Method of preparing solution of insecticides/pesticides	1.056	V
6.	Trade name of insecticides/pesticides	0.903	VI
7.	Place of availability of insecticides and pesticides	0.895	VII

20.9.2.8 Information Needs about Plant Protection Measures

During rice cultivation many problems of heavy infestations of insects and diseases are being faced by the farmers. Due to this problem many a time, expected production in rice is not possible. There are many incidences recorded of total failure of rice crop in the area of study during past years. The control of pest and diseases is most important and foremost area of information needs expressed by the rice growers as seen in the result of Table 13. Thus detail needs in this matter were studied and presented in Table 21. It was observed from the same table that majority of the rice growers have expressed their information needs about identification, nature of damage and control measures for insects/pests as well as diseases of rice crop; price of insecticides/pesticides; integrated pest management and method of preparing solutions of insecticides/pesticides.

The probable reason for information needs about identification, nature of damage and control measures for insects/pests as well as diseases of rice might be that this crop faces major problems in this regard and if plant protection is not done correctly, that may decrease production increase the cost of cultivation.

20.9.2.9 Information Needs about Harvesting and Post Harvest Technology

The information needs of rice growers about harvesting and post harvest technology were identified and presented in Table 22. It shows that Proper time of harvest, Ideal thrasher for thrashings rice, How to store rice production, Care after harvesting at farm level and Care during harvesting were major information needs of rice growers about harvesting and post harvest technology.

Table 22: The Respondents According to Information Needs about Harvesting and Post-harvest Technology

n = 100

Sl.No.	*Areas of Information*	*Mean Score*	*Rank*
1.	Proper time of harvest	1.21	I
2.	Ideal thrasher for thrashings rice	1.17	II
3.	How to store rice production	1.09	III
4.	Care after harvesting at farm level	0.92	IV
5.	Care during harvesting	0.34	V

20.9.2.10 Information Needs about Marketing

In India, production is not a problem. Modern Indian farmers have realized that with the adoption of modern practices of crop higher production is possible and as a result of such realization India has achieved significant improvement in food grain production during last few years. The major helplessness, which Indian farmers are facing, is marketing of their products. Until and unless they will not have information regarding marketing intelligence, they will not get reasonable prices of their commodities. Without having good information as regards to where to market, marketing procedure and how to get best price of their produce, they cannot fetch best price for their produce. So far as marketing decision is concerned, the place of market information is inevitable. Information needs of the respondents about marketing were documented and presented in Table 23. The rice growers expressed high information need for almost all the areas of market information. They articulated high need for information on market price followed by quality parameters that affects price and time of market inflow. The fluctuation in price of rice is very common mainly due to time of inflow, quality of rice and its' demand. Further, considerable variations between market yards are also observed. These leads rice growers to confirm high interest in the information regarding market so as to get maximum returns of their produces.

Table 23: The Respondents According to Information Needs about Marketing

n = 100

Sl.No.	*Areas of Information*	*Mean Score*	*Rank*
1.	Market price	1.79	I
2.	Quality parameters that affects price	1.72	II
3.	Time of market inflow	1.67	III
4.	Place of marketing	1.52	IV
5.	Marketing procedure	1.41	V
6.	Facilities available at market	1.21	VI
7.	Value addition	o.51	VII

20.9.2.11 Information Needs about Supportive Facts

In addition to the key areas discussed earlier, information regarding weather, government policy, credit facilities, crop insurance and subsidies etc., supportive facts were also considered as key areas for information need. Hence, information needs of the respondents were ascertained about supportive facts related to rice cultivation and presented in Table 24. It can be seen that the rice growers expressed their needs for information about subsidies, insurance and government policies related to rice cultivation. The high cost of cultivation might have led the respondents to get information about subsidies. Similarly, high risk associated with the crop may force them to acquire information of insurance. The market price of rice depends greatly on government policies, which lead the farmers to know more about government policies including support price related to rice crop, declared from time to time.

Table 24: The Respondents According to Information Needs about Supportive Facts

n = 100

Sl.No.	*Areas of Information*	*Mean Score*	*Rank*
1.	Weather forecast	0.556	V
2.	Rice related government policies	1.040	III
3.	Credit/loan facilities for rice cultivation	0.895	IV
4.	Insurance of rice crop	1.161	II
5.	Subsidies for rice cultivation	1.339	I

20.9.2.3 Correlation between Characteristics of the Rice Growers and their Information Need

Personal, social-communicational, economical and psychological characteristics of rice farmers play very important role in exhibiting information need for successful farming. With this in view, efforts were made to study the correlation between personal traits of the rice growers and their information need. To examine this relationship, correlation coefficient (r) was computed, the results of which are presented in Table 25.

20.9.2.3.1 Age and Information Need

The data presented in Table 25 clearly indicate that information need of the rice growers had non-significant correlation with their age. This might be due to fact that majority of respondents (55.65 per cent) were from the same middle age group.

Hence, the null hypothesis (H1) in case of age was accepted and it can be concluded that age of rice growers has no relationship with their information needs.

20.9.2.3.2 Education and Information Need

The data offered in Table 25 clearly signify that information need of the rice growers had non-significant correlation with their education. This may be due to the fact that irrespective level of education level of the rice growers had information need for rice cultivation remained indifferent. Thus, the null hypothesis (Ho) in case of education was accepted and it can be concluded that age of rice growers has no relationship with their information needs.

Table 25: Correlation between Characteristics of Rice Growers and Information Need

n = 100

Sl.No.	*Personal Traits*	*Correlation Coefficient Value*
1.	Age	0.011
2.	Education	0.141
3.	Use of information sources	0.192*
4.	Social participation	0.134
5.	Extension participation	0.281*
6.	Size of land holding	–0.021
7.	Land under rice cultivation	0.481*
8.	Irrigated area to total land	0.052
9.	Annual income	–0.112
10.	Cosmopoliteness	0.193*
11.	Economic motivation	-0.040
12.	Market orientation	–0.114

*: Significant at 0.05 per cent level of probability

20.9.2.3.3 Use of Information Sources and Information Need

It is evident from Table 25 that information need of the rice growers had significant correlation with their extent of utilization of information sources. This means that those rice growers who utilize more information sources to acquire information regarding rice cultivation, have shown higher need for such information. This may be due to the fact that those who were using various sources of information might have understood importance of information regarding rice cultivation. For this reason, the null hypothesis (Ho) in case of use of information sources was rejected and it can be concluded that use of information sources of rice growers has positive and significant relationship with their information needs.

20.9.2.3.4 Social Participation and Information Need

The data in Table pointed out that social participation of the rice growers had non-significant correlation with their information need. It means social organizations of villages failed to motivate rice growers to decide difference between what is and what should be for higher production of rice. That's why, the null hypothesis (Ho) in case of social participation was accepted and it can be said that level of social participation of rice growers had no relationship with their information needs.

20.9.2.3.5 Extension Participation and Information Need

It is obvious from the result in the same table that the information need of the rice growers had significant correlation with their level of extension participation. It means that extension agencies played pivotal role in identifying rice growers' information needs. The probable reason for this might be that extension activities have been considered as an important source for getting information regarding agriculture and certainly by those farmers, who were inquisitive to obtain information, took active part in extension activities. Therefore, the null hypothesis (Ho) in case of extension participation was rejected and it can be concluded that extension participation of rice growers has positive and significant relationship with their information needs of the rice growers about rice cultivation.

20.9.2.3.6 Size of Land Holding and Information Need

The Table 25 illustrates that information need of the rice growers had non-significant correlation with their size of land holding. It shows that there were all most similar needs of the rice growers with small, medium and big size of land holdings. The probable reason might be that irrespective of the size of land holding, the rice growers always try to get maximum returns from their available resources. Further, the crop being profitable one, the farmers required to be updated with latest information that leads to stability in information need irrespective to the size of holding. Thus, the null hypothesis (Ho) in case of size of land holding was accepted and it was concluded that size of land holding of rice growers has no relationship with their information needs.

20.9.2.3.7 Land under Rice Cultivation and Information Need

The data accessible in same table suggest that information need of the rice growers had significant correlation with the proportionate land under rice cultivation of their total land. The cultivation of rice crop is uncertain and it requires weighty familiarity about rice cultivation technology including plant protection measures, irrigation management, and fertilizer management. The farmer, who covers big portion of his total land under rice cultivation, transmits more risk for this crop, which leads them to have more information to minimize risk factors. This may be the reason for above finding. As a result, the null hypothesis (Ho) in case of proportionate land under rice cultivation was rejected and it was concluded that rice growers having high share of total land under rice cultivation has higher information needs.

20.9.2.3.8 Irrigated Area to Total Land and Information Need

It is apparent from the data in Table 25 that information need of the rice growers had non-significant correlation with their proportionate irrigated area to total land. This shows that any increase in irrigated area has no influence over information need of the rice grower. Hence, the null hypothesis (Ho) in case of irrigated area to total land was accepted and it can be concluded that proportionate irrigated area to total land of rice growers has no relationship with their information needs.

20.9.2.3.9 Annual Income and Information Need

The data in Table 25 point out that information need of the rice growers had non-significant correlation with their annual income. It means tat there was similar level of interest to have information on rice among rich and poor rice growers. The rice growers, with irrespective of annual income, will always have interest to increase their income that this factor might have led them to have information need for the rice cultivation technologies. Consequently, the null hypothesis (Ho) in case of annual income was acknowledged and it can be concluded that annual income of rice growers has no relationship with their information needs

20.9.2.3.10 Cosmopoliteness and Information Need

It is evident from the data in Table 25 that information need of the rice growers had significant correlation with their level of cosmopoliteness. The farmers with high level of cosmopoliteness tend to avail required information, which ultimately leads to less information need. Hence, the null hypothesis (Ho) in case of cosmopoliteness was rejected and it can be concluded that level of cosmopoliteness of rice growers has relationship with their information needs.

20.9.2.3.11 Economic Motivation and Information Need

There was information need of the rice growers had non-significant correlation with their level of economic motivation. This may be due to the similarity in term of economic motivation among those entire farmers who were growing rice. Accordingly, the null hypothesis (Ho) in case of economic motivation was time-honored and it was concluded that level of economic motivation of rice growers has no relationship with their information needs

20.9.2.3.12 Market Orientation and Information Need

It is noticeable from the Table that information need of the rice growers had non-significant correlation with their level of market orientation. The farmers growing rice crop were all most similar kind of market orientation. It is also obvious that, all the rice growers want information of rice cultivation, irrespective of their orientation to market. For this reason, the null hypothesis (Ho) in case of market orientation was accepted and it can be concluded that level of market orientation of rice growers has no relationship with their information needs

20.10 Findings

20.10.1 Characteristics of Rice Growers

1.1 From this research it can be concluded that majority of the rice growers had middle age(52.00 per cent), up to secondary to higher secondary level of education (56.00 per cent),used fertilizer depot,neighbors and television as sources of information, low to medium level of social participation (74.00 per cent), medium level of extension contact(52.00 per cent), big size of land holding(53.00 per cent), 65 per cent of their total land holding under rice cultivation(64.00 per cent), 65 per cent of their total land under irrigation (66.00 per cent) and 50,000 to 10,000 rupees of annual income (52.00 per cent), while slightly more than two fifth of the rice growers had medium level of cosmopoliteness (42.00 per cent), economic motivation (41.00 per cent) and market orientation (45.00 per cent).

20.10.2 Information Needs of the Rice Growers

2.1 Plant protection measures, Marketing, Schedule of water supply by Canal, Fertilizer management, Water management, Preparation of Seedlings, Variety, Land preparation and sowing, Supportive facts, Harvesting and post harvesting technology and Weed management.

2.2 Major information needs of rice growers about improved verities were sources of seeds, suitable high yielding variety for the area and rate of seeds.

2.3 The Information about water to be supplied in channel before sowing time and advance information about time and date of supply of water in canal for complete crop period were the expected information needs of the rice growers relate for the canal irrigation mangers.

2.4 How to select site for raising seedlings, Method of preparing bed for nursery, Plant protection in nursery management, Nutrient management in nursery, Irrigation management in nursery and Proper age to select seedlings for transplanting were the major information realized by the rice growers for nursery management in rice cultivation.

2.5 The major areas information needs expressed by the rice growers about sowing of rice were land preparation, Soil treatment methods. Place of availability of soil treatment inputs, Seed rate, Price of soil treatment inputs, Sowing time, Depth of sowing, Method of sowing, Spacing, Seed treatment inputs and Gap filling.

2.6 The major area of information needs related to fertilizer management were Price of fertilizers, Stock of fertilizers, Place of availability of fertilizers, Name of highly advantageous chemical fertilizers for rice, Method and time of fertilizer application, Nutrient requirements of plant, Calculating the doze of chemical fertilizer, Deficiency symptoms of major plant nutrients, Bio-fertilizers and procedure of making organic fertilizers.

2.7 Some of the smallest amounts of information needs expressed by rice growers for weed management were Chemical weed control, Price of weedicides, Place of availability of weedicides, Trade name of weedicides, Stock of weedicides and Hand weeding.

2.8 The rice growers expressed that Schedule for irrigation, Critical Stages of Irrigation, How to save crop during shortage of water, Fertilizer management during irrigation and Method of irrigation were key areas of their information needs regarding irrigation management in rice crop.

2.9 The major rice information needs about plant protection measures expressed by rice growers were identification, nature of damage and control measures for insects/pests as well as diseases of rice crop; price of insecticides/pesticides; integrated pest management and method of preparing solutions of insecticides/pesticides.

2.10 How to store rice production, Care after harvesting at farm level and Care during harvesting were major information needs of rice growers about harvesting and post harvest technology.

2.11 Rice growers articulated high need for information on market price followed by quality parameters that affects price and time of market inflow.

2.12 The rice growers expressed their needs for information on supportive facts like subsidies, insurance in rice crop and government policies related to rice cultivation.

20.10.3 Relationship between Characteristics of the Rice Growers and their Information Needs

3.1 The characteristics like Use of information sources, Extension participation, Land under rice cultivation and Cosmopoliteness were significantly related with their information needs for rice cultivation. In other words rice growers who had better contact with sources of information, extension personals and more area under rice cultivation as well as high level of cosmopoliteness realized more information on various aspects of rice cultivation.

Areas of Information *Month*								
Land preparation and Soil treatment								
Nursery management for seedling of pants								
Organic manure								
Variety								
Seed, Seed rate, Seed treatment								
Sowing, Spacing, Gap filling								
Nutrient requirements of plant								
Chemical fertilizer								
Bio-fertilizers								
Fertilizer application								
Integrated pest management								
Insecticides and pesticides								
Control of insects/pests								
Disease control								
Chemical weed control								
Schedule and method for irrigation								
Time and method of harvesting								
Care during and after harvesting								
Marketing								
Weather forecast								
Rice related Govt. policies								
Credit/loan facilities								
Insurance of Rice crop								
Subsidies for Rice cultivation								

References

Anonymous (2004) India, International Year Of Rice, 2004, http://www.fao.org/rice2004/en/p6.htm

Anonymous (2003) Rice – History, http://www.porkpeople.com/accomrice_history.html

Chauhan, N.M. (2011).Information on the pay attention of the rice growers. Agriculture Update, Vol-6, Issue (3 and 4), Aug and November, 2011, PP: 164-166.

Chauhan, N.M. (2012).Information Hungers of the rice growers. *Agric. Update*, vol.7 (1 and 2):72-75.

Dolli, S. S. and Sundaraswamy, B. (1994). Influence of socio-economic factors on technological gap in cultivation of pulse crop. *Maha J.Extn.Edn.* 13, PP: 175-170.

Hanuman, L.; Mundra, S. N.; Bareth, L. S. (1997). Information need of tribal and non-tribal farmers participated in rural agriculture fair. *Maha.J. of Ext.Edn*,Vol.XVI, PP:25-29.

Meera, S. N.; Jhamtani, A. and Rao, D. (2003). An analysis of agricultural information communication technology projects in India: Implications to the Agricultural Extension System. National workshop on ICT in Agriculture and Rural Development, DA-IICT; Gandhinagar, during 18-19, December 2003.

Patel, D.D (2004) Information nedd of the cotton growers, Unpublished M. Sc. (Agri.) thesis, A.A.U, Anand.

Pawar, S. P.; Sawant, P. A. and Nirban, A. J. (2001). Agriculture information needs of neo-literate farmers from Sindhudurg District. *Maha. J. Of Ext. Edn*. Vol. XX, PP:53-55.

Raut, S. S.; Tawde, N. D. and Chaudhari, D.P. (1995). Influence of the characteristics of young farmers on their training needs about cultivation of fruit crops. *Maha. J. Extn. Edn.* 11 : 292 – 294.

Saini, G. S. (1981). Information needs of the small and marginal farmers of Punjab state. *Ind.J.Ext.Edn.*, Vol.XVII(3 and 4). PP: 101-102.

Samantha, R. R. (1977). Astudy of some agro-economic, socio-psychological and communication variables associated with repayment behaviour of agricultural credit users of Nationalised banks. Unpublished Ph. D. (Agri.) thesis, IARI, New Delhi.

Sankar Rao, A. B. and Reddy, M. S. (1997). Information need of tribal farmers towards mango production technology. *Maha J of Extn. Edn.*,Vol. XVI, PP: 78-81.

Satpathy, P. K. (1995). Assessment of training needs of potato growers of Kheda district of Gujarat state. Unpublished M. Sc. (Agri.) thesis, G.A.U., Anand campus, Anand.

Singh, S. P.; Hudde, R. S. and Varma, H. K. (1991). Knowledge gap of citrus growers *Ind. J.Ext.Edn.*32 (1 and 2) PP : 117.

Singh, R and Aggarwal, P. L. (1993). Information needs of Punjabi farmwomen. *Ind. J. Ext. Edn.*, Vol.XXIX(1 and 2),PP:50-54

Stevens, J. B. and Koch, B. H. (1990). Information needs of peach farmers in Silveston Extension Ward. *South –African Jouranal of Agril Extension.* (19), PP: 7-14.

Supe, S. V. (1969). Factors related to different degrees of rationality in decision making among farmers. Unpublished Ph. D. (Agri.) thesis, IARI, New Delhi.

Talati, J. P. (1991). Training needs of banana growers of Kheda district of Gujarat state. Unpublished M. Sc. (Agri.) thesis, G.A.U., Anand.

Vaghela, D. M. (1996). Training needs of banana growers in Anand taluka of Kheda district of Gujarat state. Unpublished M. Sc. (Agri.) thesis, G.A.U., Anand.

Appendices

Interview Schedule for Measurement of Participation of the Tribal Farmwomen in Livelihood Actions

Respondent's No. : ________________ Date of interview: ________________

Village: ________________________ Taluka: ________________________

Part – I
Personal and Socio-Economic Characteristic

1. **Name:** ____

2. **Age (years completed):** ________________________

3. **Education level:** ________________________

   (a) Illiterate

   (b) Literate

4. Occupation:

   (a) Household + Farming + Agricultural labour

   (b) Household + Farming + Animal husbandry

5. Herd size:

   (a) Not owning an animal

   (b) Owning upto 2 animals

   (c) Owing 3 to 5 animals

   (d) Owing above 5 animals

6. Land holding

   (a) Marginal (up to 2.00 hectares)

   (b) Small (1.1 to 2.00 hectares)

   (c) Medium (2.1 to 4.00 hectares)

   (d) Large (Above 4.00 hectares)

7. Family size

   (a) Small family (up to 5 members)

   (b) Medium family (6 to 8 members)

   (c) Large family (above 8 members)

8. Family type

   (a) Nuclear type

   (b) Joint type

9. No of children

   (a) No child

   (b) Upto 2 children

   (c) 3 to 5 children

   (d) Above 5 children

10. Age at marriage

    (a) Age at marriage 18 years of below

    (b) Age at marriage above 18 years

Part - II
Frequency of Participation of Tribal Farmwomen in Agriculture and Animal Husbandry Practices

(A) Farming Operation

Sl.No.	Farming Operation	Participation			
		Most Frequent	Frequent	Rarely	Never
1.	Ploughing/land preparation				
2.	Clod crushing				
3.	Stubble collection				
4.	Manuring				
5.	Preparation of seedbed				
6.	Sowing/transplanting				
7.	Banding after sowing				
8.	Gap filling				
9.	Weeding				
10.	Hoeing with hand				
11.	Application of fertilizers				
12.	Spraying of insecticides				
13.	Irrigation				
14.	Bird searing				
15.	Harvesting				
16.	Making threshing yard				
17.	Nipping/picking and threshing				
18.	Bagging and packing				
19.	Marketing				
20.	Storage of farm produce				
21.	Keeping accounts/giving wages to labours				

(B) Animal Husbandry Activities

Sl.No.	*Animal Husbandry Activities*	*Participation*			
		Most Frequent	*Frequent*	*Rarely*	*Never*
1.	Cutting and bringing fodder				
2.	Watering and feeding to animal				
3.	Bathing to cattle				
4.	Shed cleaning				
5.	Milking				
6.	Preparation of milk products (Ghee, curd etc.)				
7.	Compost making				
8.	Selling of milk and its product				
9.	Taking cows and buffaloes for bull service				
10.	Taking animals for veterinary services				
11.	Grazing				
12.	Any				

Part – III
Tribal Farmwomen's Involvement in Decision-Making Process

(A) Home Management

Sl.No.	*Home Management*	*Participation*			
		Only Self	*Husband*	*Alongwith Husband/ Family Members*	*Not Related*
1.	Construction new house				
2.	Decoration of house				
3.	Children's education				
4.	Children's occupation				
5.	Children's marriage				
6.	House repair				
7.	Purchasing of household articles				
8.	Selling and purchasing of ornaments				
9.	Selection and preparation of food				
10.	Borrowing money for home management				
11.	Repayment of loan				
12.	Manner of saving				

(B) Farm Management

Sl.No.	*Farm Management*	*Participation*			
		Only Self	*Husband*	*Alongwith Husband/ Family Members*	*Not Related*
1.	Deciding area to be sown under different crops				
2.	Introduction of a new crop variety				
3.	Selection of seed				
4.	When to irrigate fields				
5.	Quantity and type of fertilizers used on the farm				
6.	Using plant protection measures				
7.	Hiring farm labours				
8.	Buying farm machinery / equipment				
9.	Installing oil engine and electric motor				
10.	Buying and selling of land				
11.	Borrowing money for farm operations				
12.	Selling of surplus farm produce				

(C) Animal Husbandry

Sl.No.	*Animal Husbandry*	*Participation*			
		Only Self	*Husband*	*Alongwith Husband/ Family Members*	*Not Related*
1.	Selection of animal breed				
2.	Selection of fodder and feed				
3.	Sale and purchase of animals				
4.	Sale and milk and its products				
5.	Keeping size of herd				

Index

V

W

Y